THE
MATADOR
THE LIFE AND CAREER OF TONY CURRIE

E.J. HUNTLEY

First published by Pitch Publishing, 2015

Pitch Publishing
A2 Yeoman Gate
Yeoman Way
Durrington
BN13 3QZ
www.pitchpublishing.co.uk

A CIP catalogue record is available for this book from the British Library.

ISBN 978-1-78531-048-5

Typesetting and origination by Pitch Publishing

Printed by TJ International, Cornwall, UK

Contents

Introduction

"Football is not really about winning, or goals, or saves or supporters. It's about doing things in style, doing them with a flourish. It's about going out to beat the other lot, not waiting for them to die of boredom."
— Danny Blanchflower

FOR many people Tony Currie was the most complete and most compelling English midfield co-ordinator of the seventies. Currie could dictate the pace of a game, could pass the ball long or short with either foot, could surge past opponents with deceptive speed and contemptuous ease; he was strong, athletic and extremely difficult to dispossess in full flow, his long, blond hair flowing in his wake and his shirt flapping outside his shorts, and what's more he could score the kind of goals that mortal players could only dream about, and could even find the time to blow kisses to the crowd following particularly extravagant pieces of showboating, frequently taunting opponent with his mastery of possession and control. If anyone could be described as the footballing equivalent of PT Barnum in the 1970s it was Tony Currie;

wherever he played, he increased the gate. Currie was a footballing matador; and Bramall Lane, and later roads Elland and Loftus were his bullrings.

His artistry and showmanship earned him a gold laminated pass into that exclusive club of impossibly gifted but mercurial English footballers who are nowadays collectively referred to as "the mavericks".

While it seems misplaced to give such individualists a collective noun there was much these Englishmen – Currie, Charlie George, Stan Bowles, Alan Hudson, Rodney Marsh, Peter Osgood and Frank Worthington – had in common; primarily their belief in football as an entertainment industry, their ability to make the game look beautiful, their popularity on the terraces and the fact that all were largely ignored by their country, particularly when Don Revie was in charge. Revie dished out 356 caps during his 29 games in charge of the national team. To the eternal dismay of most observers only eight fell into the hands of the mavericks.

While Currie shared the rock star appearance, the extravagant skills and charisma of his fellow mavericks he did not share their varied personal issues or excesses: he was no gambler like Bowles (and largely didn't share Bowles' self-destructive penchant for bad publicity), was no womaniser like Osgood, didn't share Hudson or George's combustible temperaments, didn't live life in the same fast lane as Frank Worthington and nor was he an incorrigible public show-off like Marsh.

Currie, as shy a man off the pitch as he was flamboyant on it, is adamant that his reputation as a footballing maverick was unjustified. "It was just the hair," he says. "Everyone thought they knew what I was like, just from the way I looked and played. I weren't like that at all. I was a family man."

Whilst Currie's 17 caps for England was a comparative sackful compared to the tallies received by his fellow mavericks, especially since he spent such a large portion of his career at what London sportswriters are fond of terming "an unfashionable club", it was still a desultory amount for one so gifted.

After Sir Alf Ramsey gave Currie his third cap for England – against Italy in 1973 – *The Times* praised Currie's performance and commended his, "moments of lazy Brazilian quality". A brilliant international future seemed to beckon.

Unfortunately while Currie devotees concentrated on his "Brazilian quality", Currie's detractors preferred to focus on the "L" word.

While the lazy tag would dog him throughout his career, it was frequently a misconception based on Currie's languid, graceful mode of movement and the fact that even from a young age he made the game look so easy.

In addition to the lazy tag, it was rumoured that Currie was a poor trainer and lacked dedication. While such allegations dogged Currie throughout his career none appear to contain a grain of truth. Making the game look simple was Tony's forte; his skills were effortless and his movements were languid. Currie was driven by a need for perfection that frustrated him and put him off his game when he failed to attain it. A lack of dedication had nothing to do with it.

While even the most ardent Currie supporter would concede that he was not always consistent, there were many mitigating factors. The 1970s might have been the era of the maverick but it was also an era prowled by some of the finest hard men English football has ever produced, Tommy Smith, Ron "Chopper" Harris and Norman Hunter to name but three. Additionally, since squad rotation in this era was the stuff of a madman's dreams, Currie was often forced to play when far from 100% fit *and* on pitches churned up like farmyards. It wasn't always easy to be consistent. Besides, as Danny Blanchflower once noted, "Only mediocrity is consistent."

While there are those who believe Currie failed to fulfil his potential, thus falling into that perverse and, in my view, peculiarly British trait of focusing on what someone *didn't* achieve, rather than celebrating what they did, it is my view that, over the course of his 18-year professional career that spanned over 600 games between 1967 and 1985, that Currie fulfilled his potential and more.

It's true that he never played in Europe, but that was only by ill-fortune; it's also true that he never played in a major tournament for England but that was because England failed to qualify for any of them during his heyday, and while he never won any major domestic honours he did come close on several occasions despite the fact he spent the majority of his career at "unfashionable clubs" or teams in decline.

He was without doubt one of the finest passers of a football England has ever produced, was widely regarded as a midfield genius and was idolised by the supporters who flocked to see him play. It is rumoured that in his 1970s pomp undergraduates chose to study at Sheffield's University and Polytechnic just so they could watch Currie play every other week. Indeed it is a measure of his contribution to the game that his name still carries such resonance – with the supporters of the clubs he played for and with neutrals alike.

And yet, while Osgood (*Ossie: King of Stamford Bridge*), Bowles (*Stan Bowles: The Autobiography*), Marsh (*Priceless: My Autobiography*), George (*My Story*), Worthington (*One Hump or Two?*), and Hudson (*The Working Man's Ballet*) have all written, or at least put their names to, autobiographies (which in some cases sit beside other tomes celebrating their careers on the book shop shelves), it was the fact that Currie had not been similarly honoured that inspired the first edition of this work, entitled *A Quality Player: The Life and Career of Tony Currie*, back in 2007. *The Matador*, revising, updating, expanding and hopefully improving upon that original work, puts the facts of Currie's life and career back into print where it belongs.

1

Early Days

"Me and my mates were all football crazy.
I'd dash in from school with my brother
Paul, have some tea, then we'd be off
down the park, playing 20-a-side football
until it got dark."

– Tony Currie

ANTHONY William Currie was born on New Year's Day 1950 in Edgware General Hospital in North London.

Tony was only four years old when his father, Bill, a storekeeper with Simms Motor Units, and an amateur boxing star, walked out of the family home.

With Bill Currie out of the picture, Tony's mum took Tony and his younger brother Paul to live in a three-storey house in Cricklewood, a menagerie shared by his aunts, grandparents and three uncles – Bert, Jim and Terry.

Although the break-up of a marriage is invariably traumatic for children, Tony was later philosophical about the upheaval: "Not having a father as such must

13

have had some kind of effect on me over the years but I never lacked love and affection. Times were hard but me and my brother were always dressed well and fed while the others went without."

If anything, Tony and his brother found their new environment possessed a surfeit of love and affection, having effectively swapped one father figure for three, in the shape of three uncles. Uncles Bert, Jim and Terry doted on their nephews and passed on their immense passion for football, teaching the boys skills in the garden, taking them to matches and watching them whenever they turned out for their school teams. Indeed, when asked who was the biggest influence on his career Currie replied without hesitation: "My uncles. I was a bit shy and they gave me confidence." Uncles Bert and Jim would watch every game of their nephew's career.

"My uncle Bert was the one who really raised us," Currie later expounded. "He used to take me to Stamford Bridge and we'd stand in the Shed watching Greavsie and Tambling and Bridges.

"In fact, I cried as an eight-year-old when [Greaves] moved to Italy. Jimmy was the greatest goalscorer ever and that includes Pele."

Although Currie would find fame as a midfielder, it was Greaves whom he most wished to emulate and it was he who the young Londoner would pretend to be during the 20-a-side games he would play every night with his mates on the local parks. "When I was a young hopeful living in Edgware," Tony acknowledges, "I was a Chelsea fanatic, and hero-worshipped Greaves. He could beat people easily and turn the slightest chance into a goal. Surely he was one of the greatest players of all time."

When the uncles weren't around the two boys would hone their control by bouncing a tennis ball off the roof slates and continued their soccer education with regular trips to watch nearby Hendon FC. It was whilst watching the non-league outfit that Tony learned, from scrutinising Hendon's left-winger Miles Spector, what later became known as the "Currie shuffle" – wherein Tony would flick the ball with his right foot and feint to the right, then take the ball past opponents with the other foot.

Currie, by his own admission, did not excel academically at school, but his sporting prowess was evident from an early age.

Indeed, when Currie was only eight years old his schoolteacher called at his home to seek permission for him to play in the school's under-11s team.

Such was Currie's all-round footballing ability that, initially, no one could decide which position was his best. "As a schoolboy I played in various positions for Childs Hill Junior School in the under nines, tens, elevens sides," Tony remembers, "but settled down at inside-forward with the eleven-year-olds. But when I moved to Whitefield Secondary Modern at Cricklewood I played left-half in the minor, intermediate and senior teams – and for Hendon Boys for three seasons."

Powerfully built for his age (his nickname at school was Chub) and blessed with an astute football brain, Tony was the star of the school team and remembers his time playing for Whitefield with great fondness: "We had a good side and one of the teachers, Les Hill, gave me a lot of good advice. My happiest memories are of winning two schools cup finals at Hendon... Playing at the local stadium in those games was just as big a thrill [as later playing at Wembley]."

Tony was actually operating in central defence when he was spotted, aged 14, by scouts from Queens Park Rangers. Currie duly signed amateur forms for the R's and played as a left-half in one of their junior sides. "They put me in the half-back line," Currie recalls, "but I think they decided I was too small to make a defender and they didn't move me to any other position."

Unfortunately, despite playing in a few A and B fixtures for the Hoops, Tony failed to make the grade at Loftus Road and having left Whitefield School aged 15, Tony began work as a general factotum for a building firm.

"When I left school [QPR] didn't think I was good enough to sign as an apprentice," Tony recollects. "Instead, they signed Bob Turpie who was a mate of mine and went to the same school as me. So I then had to go and work for a small building firm. I did that for six months. I was painting, decorating and plumbing from eight o'clock in the morning until six at night. I was only on a fiver a week and I didn't really enjoy the work."

Tony continued to play football, though, turning out for a local Sunday League club called Kiwi United and it was during this period that Tony was spotted by Chelsea and offered a trial. Once again, however, Currie was played out of position.

"It was a great thrill to set foot on the Stamford Bridge turf," Tony recalls. "I played in three or four trial matches, but they always seemed to want to make me into a centre-half where I was trying to mark much bigger and taller lads. It seems foolish now, but at the time I didn't have the nerve to ask them to try me out somewhere else."

As a result Tony inexplicably failed to make a sufficient impression to warrant being offered terms: "It was particularly disheartening when Chelsea turned me down because they have always been my favourite club," he explains. "I really thought it was the end of my career."

Indeed, Currie later claimed that in the six months that followed this second rejection he had all but given up the idea of playing football for a living. Currie continued to play football for Hendon Boys on Sundays, and it was during one Hendon League game that the 16-year-old Currie caught the eye of Frank Grimes, the youth coach at Watford, who serendipitously happened to be passing.

Grimes felt that Currie "had something which was worth keeping tabs on", and Watford duly offered him a six-week trial.

Nevertheless it was only a timely decision by Watford, then in Division Three, to extend the six-week trial into a six-month one (after Currie's father asked Ken Furphy, the Watford manager, if his son could be given a lengthier period of time in which to prove himself) that prevented Currie from slipping out of the professional game altogether.

"I spent six weeks at Watford," Currie explains, "and once again I was wondering if my career was going to come to a full stop before it had got going ... Watford decided to sign me on professional terms. I heaved a sigh of relief, because my dad had been talking about taking me away from Watford, since it seemed that things weren't going to pan out there, either."

After failing at QPR and Chelsea, Currie was determined not to let a third opportunity to make the grade slip through his fingers, and it was not long before he was wowing everyone at Vicarage Road with his undoubted ability. Indeed those who remember seeing him play for the Watford Juniors on the fields of South Oxhey recall how he would skip rather than sprint!

"I was the other midfielder in the Watford youth side with Tony before he went into the first team," recalls Currie's youth team colleague Barry Reed. "By far the best player I ever played with. I became a lawyer in the United States. He became what he was born to be, a football genius. I thought I had a future in the game until I played with Tony. I decided education was a better bet. I just wasn't in his class. My best recollection is that it was 1966-67. He had been rejected at Chelsea and it took a while for him to get his confidence back. His feelings were hurt. Remember he was only 16. Watford figured out what they had very quickly. He was the golden boy of the youth system and deserved to be. We also led the SE Counties in hair. We both had a lot back then."

It was clear that Tony was highly rated at Vicarage Road. One of Tony's appointed chores was cleaning the boss's Humber Sceptre and on one occasion, the young apprentice accidentally backed it into a wall while attempting to reverse the car out of a driveway. "I'll let you off this time," Furphy reassured him, "but promise me you'll send me two complimentary tickets when you play for England."

Whilst Tony was playing for the Watford youth team, Frank Grimes decided to switch Currie from an attacking wing-half to striker. It proved to be an inspired move and soon the goals started flowing in.

Watford's then player-manager Ken Furphy spotted the youngster's potential immediately and after Currie had served his apprenticeship, in May 1967 he was offered and accepted professional terms.

"Nobody could take the ball off him," Furphy reminisces. "We had a big car park with boarding all round so we could play non-stop football, one-twos off the wall. He'd put his foot on the ball and whenever anyone got near him he'd stick his backside out, or his shoulder."

While Tony's ability was not in question, Furphy did have some concerns about his young charge's attitude.

"He had so much confidence but at the same time he was very shy, very withdrawn. He misbehaved a lot early on, swearing during games. A referee rang me up one day and told me his language was disgraceful so I told Tony he wasn't playing for a month. That cured him because he loved to play."

After five games in the Watford reserve side at the start of the 1967-68 season (during which he scored six times), Currie was soon knocking on the door of the first team.

Six games into the 1967-68 season, Tony would get his chance. After losing four and winning only one of their first five league games, Watford were struggling near the foot of the Third Division. Furphy, who was finding it increasingly hard to play three games a week, decided he couldn't afford to delay the introduction of his precocious teenager for a moment longer.

"I first brought him on against Stoke in the League Cup [on 13th September 1967]," Furphy recalls. "We were 2-0 down and I would normally have gone up front under those circumstances, but I was 36 by then and I was so tired that, for the first time, I couldn't manage it, so we sent Tony on at inside-right and he hit the crossbar twice. We still lost, but he played so well I picked the same team the next week."

And so, on 16th September 1967, against Bristol Rovers, Tony Currie played the first league game of his long career, and scored twice – his first a header, the second a tap-in following a mazy dribble – in a thumping 4-0 win. It was, in Currie's words, "a dream debut".

Ten days later, in his third game for the Hornets, Tony netted a hat-trick in the 4-1 home win against Peterborough (who had beaten Watford 5-1 three weeks earlier, prior to Currie's debut), which Tony once described as one of the biggest thrills of his career. Incidentally, Tony's three goals formed a "Perfect Hat-Trick" – he slammed in his first with his right foot, nodded in his second after a perfectly timed run and then cracked home his third with his left foot.

When he reported to Vicarage Road the day after his exploits a surprise was waiting for him when he was presented with the match ball, signed by all his team-mates – which was seen as a placatory measure by the *Watford Observer* who reported that Currie had been upset at being selected for the Peterborough match as it clashed with a training session for the England youth team in Cleethorpes (Watford had had to ask for his release).

Despite five goals in his first two home games, Furphy was convinced Tony was far from the finished article and soon began leaving him out of away matches.

"He tended to drift out of the game for very long periods at that stage," Furphy considered, "and whenever he played in the first team he didn't seem to have the stamina to keep going for 90 minutes so we would try to fatten him up. We would leave him out of away games because it all seemed a bit much for him."

Furphy's remedy was to pack his young prodigy off to a local greasy spoon for a daily portion of steak and chips – fostering in Tony the love of food that would later earn him the nickname "Beef".

Although he has always acknowledged the "tremendous influence" Furphy had on his career, Tony resented his boss's cack-handed attempts to keep his feet on the ground.

"Ken Furphy was an arrogant man, certainly to me," Currie explains. "When I was at Watford, he said in the papers that he'd given me my chance and that he wouldn't be playing me if I wasn't scoring goals. He thought I was lazy as a young player. Perhaps it was me being young and naïve, but I was learning the game and thought I was doing okay. I used to get people calling me lazy, but I've got videos showing me winning the ball and then finishing moves off quite a few times, so I don't think I was."

Furphy may have left Currie out of the occasional away match but at Vicarage Road his young striker was virtually unstoppable and on 2 December he netted another hat-trick in Watford's 7-1 home win against Grimsby Town.

Playing at left-back that day for the Mariners was future Hornets and England boss, Graham Taylor, who would describe Watford's largest post-war league win as the worst day in his playing career: "I'll never forget that afternoon. I turned to look at the *Watford Observer* clock on that end stand and only an hour of the game had gone and we were six goals down. I never wanted a match to end so much."

With two professional hat-tricks to his name before his 18th birthday, it was inevitable that representative honours would soon come his way and Tony duly won his first England youth international cap in January 1968 against France, adding thousands to his market value.

Naturally, it wasn't long before Tony also started attracting the attention of other clubs, much to the ambitious youngster's excitement: "I began to read that bigger clubs were keeping an eye on my progress… and when you read about yourself, you start to hope; yet you daren't let your hopes become too high, in case they are demolished. Not every player tipped to reach the top has made it, by a long way."

The most frequent visitor to Hertfordshire to watch Currie was Sheffield United's manager John Harris, who had initially come to Vicarage Road to watch Watford's winger Stewart Scullion, only to have his attentions diverted by the elegant centre-forward with the blond hair. Although Harris would study Currie in action six times before making his move, he was instantly smitten.

"I really had no doubts about his ability the first time I saw him play," Harris remarked. "I saw enough then to make me realise he could become a top class player."

However, since Harris knew that he was not the only one keeping track of the young rookie, and that many of the clubs chasing Currie had deeper pockets than Sheffield United, the Blades' gaffer (who had captained Chelsea to the 1955 First Division title) was far from optimistic that he would be able to land his man: "I really didn't think I stood a chance when I looked at the managers around me in that directors' box at Watford."

While the other clubs prevaricated, Harris eventually made his move, tabling an offer of £26,500 – a week's wages for even the most mediocre Premiership players these days – for the teenager who had been playing league football for less than six months.

Despite Furphy's vociferous objection to the deal, Watford were in no financial position to turn it down, as Currie explains: "Watford needed to sell someone for a substantial fee to renew the lease on the ground, and £26,500 for me was quite a bit of money in those days".

"So I actually own Watford FC," Tony joked in 1997, "and I'm still waiting for my percentage."

Watford and Sheffield came to an arrangement whereby Currie would join the Blades once the Hornets had been knocked out of the FA Cup. By coincidence when the third round draw was announced, the two teams were pitched against each other. When the tie was played, Currie was left out of the Watford team (although his involvement in their games against Lowestoft and Hereford earlier in the competition ensured he was already cup-tied for United's eventual run to the quarter-finals), and watched the match seething with resentment, oblivious to the arrangement that had been struck between the two clubs behind the scenes. In the event, Sheffield United's 1-0 victory paved the way for Currie to join the victors.

Although Currie's stock – thanks to his goalscoring exploits and international recognition – had risen considerably since Watford and United had shaken hands on the deal to take him to Bramall Lane, Watford's chairman, Jim Bonser, evidently a man of integrity, stood by his word and honoured the original asking price.

When the move was finally put to Tony, he was given all of one night to think it over. Leaving London and his family at 18 years of age would be a massive wrench it was true, but Tony realised the prospect of top-flight football was too good to turn down.

"Despite the happy atmosphere at Watford, I felt I was not getting very far in the Third Division. Perhaps I was being impatient, but on the other hand I honestly knew I was a naturally gifted footballer and I wanted to show what I could do in top company.

"I didn't know much about the Blades, at that time, although I did realise they were a First Division club, and I hadn't a moment's hesitation about signing on the dotted line. So far as I was concerned, it was my big chance – maybe the only one I'd get. So I didn't take much persuading to move from Watford to the city of steel."

And so, on February 1st 1968, after nine goals in 18 league games, Currie left Vicarage Road with fond memories and grateful thanks. "But for Watford giving me my big chance," Tony reflected, "I would still be playing in Sunday League football and working as a part-time plumber and electrician."

Currie arrived at Bramall Lane to find his new club sliding inexorably towards relegation, ironically in the very season the club was celebrating its 50th season in the top flight.

Currie had primarily been bought to replace Alan Birchenall; a colourful character who had delighted Bramall Lane with his crowd-pleasing antics and swashbuckling skills before being sold to Chelsea in the latter months of 1967. It was the sale of Birchenall and the transfer of his strike partner Mick Jones to Leeds that many Blades fans believed was responsible for the club's slide down the table.

While replacing the popular Birchenall might have seemed a daunting prospect for a teenager, Currie was excited by the challenge. While he might have been a shy and reserved individual off the pitch, once he stepped onto a football field Tony was remarkably self-assured for one so young, and in time would prove to be just as flamboyant as his predecessor and even more popular among Unitedites.

This schizoid nature of his personality is one that Tony has nevertheless always acknowledged, and one that he believed many footballers share: "A lot of footballers are Jekyll and Hydes, off the field they're totally different to what they are on it. It's to do with confidence. I was like that. On the field nobody was more confident than I was and off it nobody was probably more insecure."

It was Currie's good fortune to arrive at a club full of model professionals, all keen to help the teenage Southerner settle in, particularly fellow new boy, 21-year-old Paddy Buckley (United's recent £30,000 signing from Wolves, with whom Currie initially shared digs) and former England international goalkeeper, Alan Hodgkinson.

"Every club seems to have its fair share of model footballers," Tony noted in the early 1970s, "but I reckon we have had more than most at Sheffield United since I joined the club. When I came here as a young player, I looked up to all of the rest but particularly to the long-serving goalkeeper, Alan Hodgkinson. From the moment I moved to Bramall Lane he gave me advice and helped to build up my confidence. I listened to anything that 'Hodgie' said with bated breath."

While Currie found it was easier to make friends in Sheffield because all his colleagues lived so close to each other and socialised together, Tony did initially suffer from homesickness and found it difficult to adapt to his new Northern environment.

"When I arrived in Sheffield the biggest problem I had was in settling down," Currie revealed. "I had often heard and read of players – particularly teenagers – being unsettled and losing form after being transferred. And just as often I wondered why. Surely it must make a young player feel good to know that a club wants him badly enough to pay a big transfer fee for him? I thought it would have given him a lot of confidence, especially if the move was to a club in a higher grade. I found out just how wrong I was when I moved from Third Division Watford to (then) First Division Sheffield United. I was delighted of course – it was a boost to my ego – but, oh dear, what a time it took me to settle down. Not with the club – but with the environment in the north country. It is entirely different from London where I was born and reared. There were times when I even had difficulty in understanding people I met who spoke with a broad Yorkshire accent. Just as I'm sure they had difficulty coping with my near-Cockney chatter. Always remembering of course, that I was only just 18 and had never travelled very far from my native Edgware. I know now just why a move can sometimes unsettle a player."

Although he had been bought initially with one eye on the future, such was United's plight that after only two games in United's reserves Currie was called up for his first team debut on a bitterly cold 26th February against Tottenham Hotspur.

For Currie it was "the type of debut every footballer dreams about." Not only did he line up against his childhood idol, Jimmy Greaves, but he ran rings round the legendary Scottish half-back Dave Mackay all evening and helped United seal a 3-2 win with a headed goal, outjumping Mike England to nod in a cross from David Munks.

Forty-five years later Currie would recall that having struggled to fully come to terms with the fact that he was rubbing shoulders with such legendary names, he barely acknowledged his goal.

"When I scored I didn't really celebrate. I just jogged back into position because I was a bit in awe of the names I was playing with and against. Great footballers like Greavsie and Alan Gilzean. I was still a teenager and it was a really big thing for someone my age to be in that sort of company.

"After the match I met Jimmy, and I remember that as one of the greatest thrills of my life."

It turned out to be a hectic and momentous week for Currie. On Wednesday 28th February he won his third England youth cap against Republic of Ireland youth at Portsmouth's Fratton Park and on Saturday 2nd March he married his fiancée, Linda, which meant he missed United's 3-1 defeat at Leicester City.

"We had arranged a wedding date for March and we did not want to cancel it," Tony explained. "But on the day of the wedding United were due to play Leicester. At the time of the transfer I didn't for one minute think that I would go straight into the first team so the problem of the wedding didn't occur to me.

"Sheffield United wanted me at Leicester … and my fiancée wanted me at Hendon. A right old predicament, believe me. The club offered to lay on fast cars for me, but it just couldn't be done so they finally gave way and the marriage went ahead – just!"

Currie was back for the next game away at Fulham on 13th March and was involved in the goal that secured for the Blades a 1-0 win. Currie admitted that United's goal owed a great deal to luck: "I was through on my own and as the keeper dived at my feet I shot, the ball hit him in the face – and into the corner of the net."

Despite four wins from their last six away games at Fulham, Wolves, Liverpool and Burnley, United's home form was woeful. The 3-2 win against Spurs would be the only victory Tony would enjoy at Bramall Lane that season as the Blades drew one and lost five of their last six home fixtures. That solitary point was secured against Liverpool on Easter Monday, during which Currie scored what he regarded as the best goal of his career to date, lashing a volley past Tommy Lawrence in front of the Kop: "From a right wing cross, the ball was headed back to me," Currie recalls with fondness. "I managed to hit it on the volley, and it cracked into the back of the net."

Particularly frustrating was the return fixture against Fulham who had already been relegated when they arrived at the Lane. Despite taking a two-goal lead United contrived to concede three goals in eleven minutes to lose the match 3-2.

Currie would later admit that it took him a while to get used to playing at Bramall Lane, which, for all but Currie's final season as a Sheffield United player, was a three-sided ground which hosted cricket during the summer.

"I only had one season with the newly built South Stand," Currie told the Sheffield United matchday programme in 2001, "so I remember [Bramall Lane] best as three-sided with the cricket pavilion in the distance. The changing rooms in the old John Street stand were dim and dingy, but they were improved within a year or so. Within a few weeks of the season starting there was a diamond shaped grassless area in the middle of the pitch, and you never knew from week to week whether it would be three inches of mud or a frozen area that had been rolled flat. It took me about a year to get used to it."

Although a mere two wins from their preceding eight games had made United relegation favourites, as they approached their last game of the 1967-68 season they still had a mathematical chance of staying up.

Sheffield United were faced with the testing but not insurmountable task of beating Chelsea at home whilst at the same time hoping either Coventry slipped up away at Southampton or Stoke City (whose goal difference was inferior) lost at Leicester.

If Coventry won and Stoke avoided defeat, only an eight-nil win would push the Blades above their rivals Sheffield Wednesday who had completed their fixtures the week before. While Stoke's draw ensured *their* safety, Coventry's draw at The Dell meant they would be down if United could beat Chelsea. Unfortunately, despite going in at the break a goal up, the Blades succumbed to a 2-1 defeat and were sent crashing down to the Second Division.

To make matters more galling, United finished only two points behind their auld enemy and fiercest rivals, Sheffield Wednesday, who stayed up with 34.

As far as Currie was concerned the Blades' relegation had more to do with the fates than with his new team's actual ability: "I felt that we were somewhat unlucky," Tony contended. "The ball just didn't run for us so too many matches were lost or drawn which we should have won. Even in the final game against Chelsea which determined our fate, we were cursed with bad luck.

Anybody who saw the side which beat West Ham in the FA Cup must have been impressed. I was cup-tied for that game, unfortunately, but any team which can play as well as we did that day does not deserve to be relegated.

"Towards the end of [the] season one or two of our fans were saying that the team was not trying. If only they knew! We did double training most days to ensure peak physical fitness and on [matchdays] we tried our hearts out, honestly."

Currie finished the season with five goals from 13 games. Despite United's relegation, it was abundantly clear that Harris had unearthed a player with tremendous potential, and his dazzling array of skills was immediately recognised and appreciated by United supporters with whom Currie would soon develop such a singular rapport.

First team coach Cec Coldwell recalls the precocious teenager was almost beyond coaching: "You'd just have to give him the freedom of the park and let him do his own thing."

Currie may have been beyond coaching but as far as Coldwell was concerned the player still needed the occasional rocket from his manager to get the best out of him: "One day John gave him a roasting, telling him that he wasn't giving his best. It was the only time I ever saw John really open up. I think it knocked Tony over. Just before the players went back out I had a chat with him and tried to lift him. It worked: he played a different game second half."

Such dressing downs, however, were the exception rather than the rule (Harris was no authoritarian) and Currie, like all of his United colleagues, had enormous admiration and respect for the man who had plucked him from Watford. "John Harris was like a quiet Bill Shankly," Tony observes. "He could have been Shankly's brother because they were both tough Scots. But the difference was that John was a private gentleman who never drank or smoked and he didn't like the limelight at all. He didn't want to talk to the press and he didn't even talk much in team meetings, leaving it more to the players. Alf Ramsey was a bit like that as well. John was always in a collar and tie, never in a tracksuit. He'd be there for every training session, walking about and observing, but he left the training to John Short who was the first team coach. Cec Coldwell later took over the role of coach."

* * * * *

Following United's relegation, Harris was given the role of general manager and Shrewsbury Town boss Arthur Rowley (the Football League's all-time record goalscorer – with 433 strikes from 619 games for West Brom, Fulham, Leicester City and Shrewsbury Town) took over as team manager in July 1968.

Rowley would not enjoy the happiest of times at Bramall Lane. Strangely for someone who had scored so many goals as a player, when he moved into management Rowley adopted a defensive, safety-first approach to tactics, particularly away from home.

After opening the 1968-69 season with four wins and a draw, the Blades quickly began to struggle in the second tier, winning just one of the ten league games that followed that bright start (losing six) and also crashed out of the League Cup, losing 4-0 away at Liverpool.

Although United returned to winning ways on 26th October with a 2-0 victory at home to Charlton Athletic, this was marred when Currie was carried off five minutes before the end of the game with a knee injury. Although the injury did not initially appear to be excessively serious in the event it would keep Tony out of action until 21st December.

"I didn't think I would be out of action as long as I was," Currie stated. "After four weeks, with trainer Harry Latham and physiotherapist Geoff Goodall putting in so much fine work, I felt quite good.

"Then for about five weeks I just could not turn on the injured knee at all. Believe me, I was fed up to the back teeth during this period, for I've never been out of the game for such a long spell before and I sincerely hope I never have to be out of the game for as long again."

In fact, Currie was so eager to play again that he returned to action too quickly. After scoring two goals for United's reserves against Bury Tony declared himself fit enough to reclaim his place in the first team (who had won three and lost three in Currie's absence) when they hosted Huddersfield four days before Christmas.

Currie was the first to admit that he was way off the pace in the goalless stalemate with the Terriers and had no complaints when he was substituted in the second half.

Although he missed the Blades' 1-1 home draw with Crystal Palace on Boxing Day the postponement of United's fixture with Charlton and another game in the reserves afforded Currie the opportunity to regain his match fitness, and on 4th January he was named as sub when the Blades travelled to play lowly Mansfield Town in the third round of the FA Cup. Unfortunately it would prove to be a day to forget as the Third Division side defied the odds and United's 1-0 half-time lead to win the tie 2-1. Not even Currie's introduction from the bench after 67 minutes could prevent United from suffering one of the club's most embarrassing ever cup defeats, a result and a frankly dismal display that heaped yet more pressure on the increasingly beleaguered Arthur Rowley.

The only consolation from the Blades' shock cup exit was that Currie suffered no negative reaction from the knee and he was able to return to United's starting line-up for the remainder of the season.

Despite Currie's recall the Blades' results remained maddeningly inconsistent. Although United would enjoy an unbeaten end to the season at Bramall Lane, the Blades won only one of their remaining ten away fixtures (losing six) to finish in a disappointing ninth place.

It wasn't so much United's final league position that cost Rowley his job (he was relieved of his duties shortly before the start of the following season), more the manner in which it had been achieved. The sale of mercurial but popular playmaker Willie Carlin, the early exits from both domestic cups and his negative approach (playing for draws away from home – they won only twice on their travels all season), did not endear him to the fans or the players and with John Harris (with whom, it was said, Rowley did not get on) looking over his shoulder from upstairs and his predecessor's coaching staff still in situ, the new man struggled to stamp his authority on his new club.

Whilst acknowledging that Rowley's cautious approach was a factor in the manager's failure to win hearts and minds, Currie also believes that Rowley did not have the rub of the green during his time at Bramall Lane.

"Arthur was also quiet," Tony reckons, "but he was different to John because he was brash. He instilled confidence in you and I got on with him well, but he perhaps just didn't get the right team together or play the right tactics. We had a good team, but we didn't have a good squad, so we struggled if anyone got injured."

To write off Rowley's time in charge as a wasted year, however, would be quite wrong. His record in the transfer market was nothing short of remarkable, bringing to Bramall Lane several of the individuals who would eventually lead Sheffield United back to the Promised Land of the First Division, including left-half Ted Hemsley (a £27,500 capture from Shrewsbury Town), West Bromwich Albion's Scottish defender Eddie Colquhoun (who arrived in October 1968 at a cost of £27,500), centre-forward John Tudor (a £58,500 buy from Coventry), Welsh international defender Dave Powell (who joined from Wrexham for £28,000) and John Flynn (who signed from Workington in July 1969 for a fee of £5,000).

Moreover, Rowley wasted little time in getting rid of players if he felt their attitude was wrong (Carlin, the Wagstaff brothers, David Munks and stalwart full-back Bernard Shaw). His legacy was a team of disciplined, committed and honest professionals who all wanted to play for Sheffield United.

Despite the soundness of his investments, Rowley's Blades failed to find a consistent run of form and when the side finished in a disappointing ninth place Rowley paid the price with his job and, in August 1969, John Harris resumed control of team affairs.

Although Tony was as anxious as anyone to return to the First Division, he regarded his spell in the second tier as an invaluable experience that was actually beneficial to his footballing development: "When I look back, I cannot say that a spell in Second Division football [did] me any harm at all – indeed I was young enough to be learning something from every game that I played."

While the 1968-69 season had been a largely barren one in front of goal for Currie (with only four goals from 35 League appearances), the return of Harris coincided with Tony rediscovering some of his scoring touch with four goals in United's first seven games of the 1969-70

33

campaign. And it was on the back of such form that Tony was rewarded, in October 1969, with the first of his 13 appearances for the England Under-23 side.

Alongside the likes of Peter Shilton, Colin Todd, Brian Kidd and Peter Osgood, Currie kept up his habit of scoring on his debut with the second goal a minute from time in England's 2-0 win against Wales. (Incidentally, Currie would also score in his second Under-23 match, in the 4-1 win against Bulgaria at Plymouth's Home Park on 8th April the following year.)

* * * * *

With Harris back in charge there were high hopes that the 52-year old Scot would repeat his successful promotion campaign of 1960-61 and guide United back to the top flight.

United started the 1969-70 campaign with seven wins, one draw and only one defeat from their first nine league and cup fixtures, a run which included a satisfying return to Vicarage Road for Currie. Not only was Tony appointed skipper for the day against his old club, he also celebrated by scoring the winning goal to send United to the top of Division Two.

In contrast to United's defensive style under Rowley, John Harris's teams played only one way – with the emphasis on attack, as a number of emphatic victories in the first half of the season bore considerable witness. In August United crushed Portsmouth 5-1 at Fratton Park (with Currie scoring twice in a minute), before putting another five past them in the return fixture in October. In November United beat both Blackburn and Aston Villa 4-0 before scoring six without reply against Birmingham in December. At the end of the season, it was results like these that earned Sheffield United an invitation to play in the inaugural Watney Cup – the short-lived but fondly remembered pre-season tournament that was open to the previous season's two top-scoring teams in each of the four divisions.

There was also concrete evidence that United could beat anybody on their day with two remarkable cup wins against First Division opponents. In September Newcastle United were dispatched in the second round of the League Cup, despite the Blades having to field Alan Woodward as an emergency goalkeeper for the final quarter of an hour (United eventually bowed out at the fourth round stage following a 2-0 defeat at Leicester). In the third round of the FA Cup, at Bramall Lane, United saw off Everton, clawing back a 1-0 half-time deficit to beat the eventual First Division champions 2-1, thanks to headed goals from Gil Reece and Colin Addison.

Inconsistency, however, was United's biggest problem. Although United were eminently capable of piecing together a sequence of wins, they were equally capable of suffering a sequence of defeats. Between 17th January and 13th March, for example, United won five out of their six league games but then promptly lost each of their next four.

Ultimately it was those four consecutive defeats in March that proved fatal to United's promotion dreams, and from looking odds-on certainties to return to the top flight earlier in the season, Sheffield United had to settle for a disappointing sixth place. Nevertheless the fact that United finished only four points adrift of second placed Blackpool represented a significant improvement and offered great hope for the following campaign.

Although 1970 was not to be United's year, Harris was carefully assembling and refining the ingredients that would not only deliver promotion but also ultimately sustain life in the top flight.

The purchase of 26-year-old journeyman striker Billy Dearden, a £10,000 steal from Fourth Division Chester City, towards the end of the 1969-70 season would prove to be a sensational piece of business, while Harris's decision to switch Ted Hemsley from a midfielder struggling to make an impression to a left-sided full-back would prove equally shrewd. In addition, the emergence of local youngsters Frank Barlow and the athletic Geoff Salmons were both great cause for optimism, with Salmons in particular looking a very useful prospect on the left side of midfield. Rowley's buys had all settled in comfortably, and with right-back Len Badger, Alan Hodgkinson, striker Colin Addison, Welsh winger Gil Reece, and Alan Woodward proving as reliable as ever, Harris seemed to have found the perfect blend.

"We began to develop into a good side," Currie recalls, "and we knew that it was only a matter of time before we would be back in the First Division."

2

1970–71

"I always felt that I was better suited to a creative role in midfield. I had a chat with Mr Harris at the beginning of our promotion season and he suggested we give it a try."
— Tony Currie

AFTER two full seasons as a striker, it was clear that Tony was not and was never likely to become a prolific and instinctive goal-poacher in the Jimmy Greaves mould.

Currie therefore decided that his vision and artistry could better serve Sheffield United's cause from the centre of midfield.

"After two seasons as a striker I realised it just wasn't my game," Currie later acknowledged. "During the close season, I had a chat with John Harris and told him I thought I might be better off making goals. 'I'd like to play in midfield because I'm coming back and making goals for everybody else,' I said. He agreed to give it a try."

The change of position would prove to be the making of Currie, transforming him from a promising young Second Division striker into an inspirational midfield schemer whom spectators flocked through the turnstiles to watch.

United's results at the start of the 1970-71 season suggest that it initially took Currie a few games to fully acclimatise to his new role. In fact, the Blades made a poor start to the campaign, winning only one of their first five matches. However, an unbeaten run of 16 league games between early September and the end of November saw the team find the kind of consistency that had eluded them the previous season.

During this run Currie found himself revelling in his new midfield berth, spraying passes long or short with both feet and surging past opponents with contemptuous ease. "I'm enjoying the freedom of playing in midfield," he remarked at the time. "It's giving me more opportunities to come forward and have a go at goal."

Tony's success in his new role was spectacularly demonstrated during United's clash with Don Revie's mighty Leeds United in the second round of the League Cup on 8th September. First Division runners-up the previous season and current league leaders Leeds were widely expected to crush their Yorkshire rivals. Instead it would be the Blades who would emerge victorious, confirming their potential to thrive in the top tier.

Prior to the match, Harris had urged his team to attack Leeds and his charges responded with a magnificent display, in which Currie in particular was outstanding. Underlining his ability to win games with one magnificent pass or breathtaking piece of improvisation, it was Currie who settled the tie with a memorable goal – showing England left-back Terry Cooper a clean pair of heels in a chase from the halfway line before unleashing an unstoppable 25-yard strike that whistled past Gary Sprake in the Leeds goal.

"We lost to the better side," Leeds' manager Don Revie graciously acknowledged after the match. "The Blades were the fastest team I've played against in years," added Norman Hunter.

Tony was delighted with the win and delighted with his goal, permitting himself the liberty of a stock football cliché during his post-match interview: "Everyone played well and when I saw that gap open up in the Leeds defence I thought I could score if I could hit the small target to Gary Sprake's left. I was over the moon when it went in."

Inspired by their win against Leeds, and with Currie pulling the strings, the Blades began putting together some highly impressive results, including a 2-1 win away at Millwall, a second 5-1 win in two years away at Portsmouth's Fratton Park (with Woodward hitting a hat-trick) and, in Currie's 100th league game for United, a thrilling 3-2 derby win against Sheffield Wednesday.

Currie's form was rewarded with a third England Under-23 cap, in a 3-1 victory against West Germany, played at Leicester City's Filbert Street ground on 14th October, and a fourth the following February in the 2-2 draw with Scotland at Hampden Park in which Tony scored and helped create another for Larry Lloyd to retrieve a two-goal deficit. Currie's goal – cleverly intercepting a back pass before finishing crisply – was his third goal in four Under-23 appearances.

In between Tony's third and fourth Under-23 appearances, meanwhile, the wheels were threatening to come off Sheffield United's promotion charge with three defeats away from home (against Luton Town, Swindon Town and Bolton Wanderers) either side of Christmas and another early FA Cup exit courtesy of a 2-0 defeat away at Portsmouth.

After the defeat at Bolton, in order to prevent a repeat of the previous season's failings, John Harris decided that his team was in urgent need of the boost that only fresh faces can bring. Harris's first area of concern was the goalkeeping department.

Having made 600 first team appearances there can be little doubt that Alan Hodgkinson had been one of Sheffield United's greatest ever players, but, after 17 years of reliable service, the keeper's judgement was starting to falter, particularly when it came to dealing with crosses. To replace Hodgkinson (who joined United's backroom staff as reserve team coach), Harris brought in Newcastle keeper John Hope who arrived with former Sheffield Wednesday midfielder David Ford as part of an exchange deal that saw John Tudor heading to St James' Park.

The unexpected departure of Tudor was a risky strategy. Not only had the popular forward already contributed nine goals that season (including the winner against Wednesday in October), he had also on occasion proved a capable deputy in the centre of defence.

The second area of concern for Harris was Sheffield United's midfield, which he believed lacked bite and aggression. Although Currie had impressed in the middle of the park, he was primarily a constructive player not a snarling destroyer. Harris's solution was to shell out £40,000 for Birmingham City's aggressive and experienced ball-winner Trevor Hockey, a converted winger.

While the arrival of new faces can often revitalise a team, it can also have an unsettling effect on a close-knit group of players, with new players taking time to settle in and gel with their new team-mates. Fortunately United's new signings assimilated quickly.

As far as Currie was concerned the arrival of three new faces on the same day was "the key to the First Division door".

"From then on we lost only two of our remaining 17 League games," he remarked, "and it was good to see the crowds flocking back."

While Hope did provide the height and authority to cope with the situations that had begun to trouble Hodgkinson, it was the determined, industrious performances of Trevor Hockey that proved decisive. With his distinctive, piratical beard, long hair and headband, Hockey was an instant success with supporters and team-mates alike, providing that elusive extra ingredient, that missing *edge* on the field and boosting the morale of the dressing room off it.

"Hockey was only 5ft 6in tall," Len Badger recalls, "but he was a hard lad whose father was a rugby league player from Keighley. If you were playing away from home and somebody was doing you a bit of damage, you could just say, 'Hock,' and he'd do a job on them. He was a real character who stood out. When we signed him from Birmingham, he arrived in a Triumph Vitesse, which was a nice car, the difference being that he'd had it covered in velvet! It was fantastic."

"The manager wanted to add a bit of steel to the team and Trevor certainly did that," adds Ted Hemsley. "Ten minutes before every game he'd jump and start shouting and screaming at all of us, including himself, and kicked lumps out of the wall. It must've worked because I don't remember us conceding a goal early on in any game."

When Hockey joined the Blades, he received only three instructions from his new boss, namely, "To battle, win the ball and give it to Currie." The rest, as far as Harris was concerned, would take care of itself.

Hockey and Currie would not only form a formidable partnership in the centre of United's midfield they would also become firm friends off the pitch.

"I'll never forget rooming with Trevor Hockey," Currie would later recall with fondness. "What an experience that was because he had the smelliest feet in the world. Trevor was absolutely bonkers but you couldn't wish to meet a nicer bloke. He had a pink piano at home and crushed velvet seats in his car."

Hope and Hockey made their debuts together in the 2-1 win away at Oxford United, with Billy Dearden scoring both goals. The following week another 2-1 win at home to Luton (which saw the introduction of Ford) and a 2-0 win at Charlton Athletic saw United briefly return to the top of the table.

With several credible candidates scrapping over only two promotion places it was inevitable that results could not always be expected to go United's way and as February 1971 gave way to March, United suffered two painful setbacks in quick succession in the shape of defeats against close rivals Carlisle and, in a bruising encounter, Hull City (which had left Currie, Badger, and Dearden all requiring treatment to get them fit for the following match – Currie having been kicked from pillar to post throughout by the Tigers' Ken Knighton) – the latter becoming the first and last opposing team to win at Bramall Lane during the 1970-71 season.

Four days following the defeat against Hull, the Blades travelled to QPR hoping to get their season back on track. In a thrilling, action-packed game Ted Hemsley twice had to clear off the line to thwart Rangers in the early exchanges, while United spurned at least two good chances at the other end. In the 23rd minute, however, United's Welsh international defender Dave Powell was forced from the field to receive treatment for a knee injury and it was while United were down to ten men, four minutes later, that Rangers took the lead through Rodney Marsh. Although United pushed hard without success for an equaliser, when Marsh added a second for Rangers on the hour, the Blades found themselves staring down the barrel of a potentially ruinous third consecutive defeat.

Even when Woodward pulled a goal back in the 88th minute it seemed likely to be little more than a consolation. However, in the dying seconds Dearden was up-ended in the penalty area by Dave Clement, and Ted Hemsley kept his nerve to convert the spot-kick to salvage another crucial point.

Although the result was marred by Dave Powell's injury (which proved so serious that he never played another league game for United) it turned out to be another turning point. After narrowly avoiding a third consecutive defeat, the Blades remained unbeaten throughout the rest of the season, concluding their campaign with four more draws and six wins.

The Blades kicked off their run-in in fine style, romping to a 5-0 home win against Blackburn (with Woodward scoring in the first minute before an opponent had even touched the ball!), followed by a 1-0 win away at Bristol City in which Currie scored the winner, coolly slotting home after a mazy run which saw him dribble past virtually City's entire team.

Despite a disconcerting run of three goalless draws (including one at Hillsborough in front of a gate of 47,500), wins against Millwall and Birmingham put the Blades back in second place with three games remaining.

After a hard-fought draw against Middlesbrough (with Hope in outstanding form), everything boiled down to United's penultimate fixture – a showdown at Bramall

Lane against their closest rivals for promotion, Cardiff City. Victory would virtually guarantee promotion for either side.

United were in second place behind Leicester City heading into the Cardiff game, one solitary point above Cardiff having played a game more than the Welsh side. The pressure was well and truly on. Fortunately, Sheffield United rose to the big occasion.

On a memorable night crackling with electricity, in front of a pumped-up crowd of almost 43,000 (Bramall Lane's biggest of the season), goals from Dearden (after six minutes) and a diving header from Flynn (on 33 minutes) put United 2-0 up. Although a Cardiff reducer in the 38th minute set Sheffield nerves a-jangling, ten minutes after the re-start a headed goal from Tony Currie, who had been at his arrogant best throughout the match, restored United's precious two-goal cushion. Currie's goal, however, was not without controversy.

"I feel United's first and third goals were illegal," Cardiff's manager Jimmy Scoular protested after the match, "and the third one should go down as an own goal as our keeper punched it in after Currie had punched him."

Fortunately Scoular's complaints were rendered academic when Gil Reece made it 4-1 after 66 minutes before Dearden's second of the evening completed a comprehensive 5-1 rout, a result which also pushed United's goal average above Cardiff's.

Despite his misgivings about the legitimacy of two of United's goals, a devastated Jimmy Scoular was magnanimous in defeat: "Defeat last night was one of the most disappointing moments of my 25 years of football. But good luck to Sheffield United. They should hold their own in the First Division."

Unaware that promotion had not in fact been secured, the United players nevertheless celebrated with a night out, as Len Badger explains: "We were so elated after the match and we went for a drink at the Penny Farthing nightclub, which was at the back of the Moor in the centre of Sheffield. By the time quarter to one came round, everybody began to think about the next game. There were about eight or nine of us there and it suddenly dawned on us that promotion hadn't yet been achieved. We knew we had to get at least a point at the weekend. Suddenly there we were thinking, 'We've got to do it all again on Saturday.'"

The Cardiff result meant United needed just one point from their last match, at home to Currie's former club Watford, to go up with Leicester who had already secured their promotion as the division's champions. The match would be Currie's 150th in league football – an impressive statistic for a 21-year-old.

Although United needed only a point to secure promotion, Harris told his players to go flat out for the win, describing the game as, "the most important match in [Sheffield United's] history."

Certainly Watford seemed up for the match. Despite languishing, albeit safe from relegation, in the bottom half of the table, and with little to play for other than professional pride, Watford manager Ken Furphy warned their opponents prior to the match that it would be foolish to underestimate his team; they were not coming to Bramall Lane merely to form the guard of honour. His team, he vowed, would come intent on winning the match.

To increase his side's chances of doing precisely that, Furphy announced that Walter Lees would be detailed to man-mark the Blades' danger man – Tony Currie – the player he had sold to United for almost £30,000 in 1968, and who, in Furphy's opinion, was "now worth double that amount!"

True to their word, Watford attacked from the off and almost took the lead on eight minutes when their talented winger Stewart Scullion smashed a volley against United's crossbar.

To the relief of the majority of the 38,857 spectators inside Bramall Lane, however, Scullion's effort proved to be nothing more than a wake-up call. In the 21st minute, Watford's Keith Eddy brought down Gil Reece in the penalty area and Alan Woodward stepped up to wallop home the spot kick, in the process scoring his 15th goal of the season. Two minutes later Woodward turned provider, threading a neat ball through to Reece who duly made it 2-0 with an emphatic finish. Two goals in two minutes effectively ended the match as a contest and when Reece added a third in the second half the celebrations could begin. United were a First Division side again.

"Nothing was going to stop us on that sunny fantastic day," Currie recalls. "The players all went up to the directors' box in John Street to wave to the crowd. My only disappointment was having one of the two shirts I wore that afternoon pinched from the dressing room at half-time. At least I still have the other."

It was, according to Currie, the highlight of his Sheffield United career: "The scenes were unbelievable. All the other lads were throwing their shirts to the crowd. I wanted to keep mine."

One of the most satisfying aspects of United's promotion was the manner in which it had been achieved. The perceived wisdom, then as now, is that the second tier of English football is such a hard division to get out of that the only way to do so is to emphasise the physical.

Although promotion had not been secured at a canter, United nevertheless had made a mockery of such a theory. They combined a deserved reputation as one of the most stylish and entertaining teams in the entire country with a strong team spirit that refused to acknowledge defeat even when the chips were down – as they had shown in the games at home to Bristol City and away at QPR.

Currie, along with Badger and Woodward, was ever-present throughout the campaign; while Colquhoun and the lion-hearted Dearden each missed only one game (the latter despite needing a cartilage operation which he postponed until promotion had been sealed at the request of his manager) and Hemsley was absent for just two.

If the settled line-up allowed the players to develop telepathic relationships in key areas, off the pitch, the players were a friendly, tightly knit bunch that got on well together, socialised together, knew each other's families and had a deep sense of feeling and loyalty towards the club and its supporters who reciprocated with interest.

"There was a great rapport with the crowd who never really got at us when we didn't play well," Ted Hemsley remembers. "You could have a laugh with someone in the crowd during a game."

No one epitomised this better than Tony Currie. The Bramall Lane faithful adored Currie's antics, particularly his trademark kisses to the crowd after a goal.

"Yes, I play to the crowds," Tony explained to John Sadler in 1973. "Why not? I only do it at the right time. Winning comes first, of course, but there are occasions when a player can show off a bit. The fans love it, anyway. Soccer is part of the entertainment industry. Hundreds of thousands of people pay big money to watch the players. And I firmly believe that a little bit of showmanship helps the game. Take my gimmick of blowing kisses when I score. I got over-emotional in one match and that's when I did it for the first time. I suppose I got carried away but the crowd liked it."

"I loved playing at the Lane and looked forward to it all week," Currie told the Sheffield United matchday programme in September 2001, "it was just fantastic to run out in front of 25,000 or so who adored you. Some players hear the crowd, others claim not to. Team-mates like Alan Woodward never reacted to the fans but I was aware of them and their shouts and found time to wave, shout back or blow a kiss! But I only ever did it when it was safe and, in any case, people like Eddie Colquhoun or Len Badger used to remind me to, 'Concentrate, TC!'"

Despite the occasional admonishments of his team-mates, it was often said that it was worth the admission price in those days just to see Currie pass the ball. While Sheffield United without doubt had several players who were exciting to watch, it was Currie that had that little bit extra, and he was widely acknowledged as the key to United's promotion, even netting nine goals in the league and 15 in all competitions. In recognition of his contribution, Tony was voted Sheffield United's Player of the Year at the end of the 1970-71 campaign.

As far as Currie was concerned the transition to midfield had proved an easy one and he generously conceded that a phalanx of talented colleagues often made him look good: "We had all these speed merchants – Alan Woodward, Geoff Salmons, Gil Reece, Bill Dearden. I could put the ball where I wanted, they just had to move."

It was Currie's blossoming understanding with Alan Woodward in particular that captured the Bramall Lane imagination. To see Woodward latching onto a raking Currie pass was an electrifying sight.

Woodward was an outside-right of the highest class, with all the attributes one might wish for in a wide player, and more besides. He was fast, strong, skilful, clever and direct, had great ball control and the ability to beat his opponent, could cross with unerring precision with either foot (his corner kicks were particularly dangerous) and had a shot like an exocet missile. On top of which he was also a prolific goalscorer – claiming a post-war record haul for Sheffield United of 175 goals in 595 games. The fact that he would never win an England cap (although he did represent the Football League) remains an enduring mystery to Blades fans, and to Tony Currie, too: "Woodward should have played for England. The fact that he didn't was just down to the fact that he was at United. If you played for a big club or one of the London clubs, you got picked. We were seen as an unfashionable club. Woody should have had a few caps at least. He was a phenomenal player who scored goals as a winger. He was a top class finisher who hit the ball powerfully with his left or right foot and was great at dead balls."

In John Harris's opinion, Woodward's only weakness, in contrast to Tony Currie, seemed to be a deficient self-belief, the Scot once remarking, "He simply has no conception of how much talent he has."

Even though it was Currie whose poster adorned the bedroom walls, the Sheffield United dressing room was no place for egos and it was not in Currie's nature to act the diva in any case. Instead the players shared a genuine camaraderie and mutual respect that for the surviving members of the promotion team exists to this very day.

Even the most cursory glance at the "Hobbies and Interests" section of the player profiles of the *Promotion Souvenir Brochure* tells you all you need to know about the temperaments and character of this particular group of professionals: Colquhoun listed reading and brass bands among his hobbies; Hockey listed reading books on archaeology, while Dave Powell was a fly-fishing enthusiast who drove a Mini Clubman! It seems light years away from the overpaid, Ferrari driving, speeding ticket dodging, Cristal glugging, toilet-seat-stealing scofflaws who *now* populate the beautiful game.

There was every reason to believe that this bunch of players would thrive upon their return to the top flight. It was a group that had been together for some time and had almost forgotten how to lose.

On the crest of this wave of optimism, the Sheffield United board finally decided, after a protracted period of petitions, votes and public debates, that Bramall Lane would no longer play host to cricket matches, and would instead be turned into a four-sided stadium, as befitting a First Division club.

Whilst there was no faulting the board's architectural ambitions, the building of what became the South Stand at Bramall Lane was nevertheless a huge gamble that would have massive implications for United's and Currie's long-term future.

3

Fear Lends Wings

*"A kind of feverish brilliance attended the
play of the United while so much depended
on the wayward talents of Tony Currie
– a histrionic player with mannerisms
characteristic of what one day will be
termed the Best era."*
– Percy M. Young *(Football in Sheffield)*

THE 1971-72 season presented Sheffield United
with a brand new challenge – namely top-flight
survival. Having emptied his war chest to bring
Hope, Hockey and Ford to the club for the promotion
run in, John Harris could afford to make only one notable
pre-season signing – Watford's Stewart Scullion who was
snapped up for a bargain £30,000.

Consequently, Sheffield United would commence
their first season back in the big time with virtually the

same nucleus of players that had secured promotion. Given the personnel at his disposal, it was inevitable that John Harris would opt to retain the policy of all-out attack. It was a brave strategy, but the men under his command were footballers for whom a season of grinding consolidation would have been anathema.

"We came up from the Second Division with a reputation for playing with intelligence and style," Harris rationalised. "We elected to go on playing that way because we felt we had a duty to the public. We are not a dainty team, but we have people who can play the game, which is what matters."

Not everyone in the Sheffield United ranks was feeling as gung-ho as their manager, however. Certainly full-backs Ted Hemsley and Len Badger recall a far from optimistic dressing room when the fixture list for the start of the season was announced. During their opening four games, the Blades would be pitched against the league champions of the previous three seasons: Leeds United, Everton and Arsenal, and the last two away from home.

"We had been promoted to the top flight and in pre-season went on tour in Holland," Hemsley recalls. "After about five days we were sore and knackered and weren't up to playing against a really top team in a full stadium. We got the biggest 2-0 hiding of our lives, hardly touching the ball all match. It frightened us to death because we then looked at our league fixture list, saw the big names coming up and wondered where we were going to get a point from! It was going to be embarrassing and we were in shock so we made our minds up to run non-stop, back each other up – fear lends wings."

"We looked at the games and saw we faced South-ampton, Leeds, Everton, Arsenal and West Brom at the start of the season," adds Len Badger. "There were only two points for a win then and we said, 'To get two points out of that would be fantastic.'"

Instead Sheffield United hit the ground running with a 3-1 win over Southampton, followed three days later by a 3-0 trouncing of old enemies Leeds United (with goals from Flynn, Dearden and Colquhoun) before a delirious crowd of over 40,000. With the latter result, any doubts about the Bramall Lane squad's ability to live in the First Division were well and truly swept away.

Another impressive 1-0 win at home to Everton was followed by a trip to Highbury and a showdown with Arsenal, the reigning league champions and FA Cup holders. It too yielded a 1-0 win. Although the swashbuckling Blades could only manage a goalless draw against West Brom in their fifth game of the season, back-to-back wins against Huddersfield and Nottingham Forest meant that United had started the season with an astonishing 13 points from a possible 14.

"We were playing some fantastic stuff and absolutely flying," Len Badger rhapsodises. "People were knocking the ball about and going round people; TC was dropping his shoulder and blowing kisses to the crowd. We had the right balance and played with no fear. It was the same home or away, with everybody fitting into the system."

"The reason for our early success was ATTACK!" Currie explained in 1973. "So many clubs expect a newly promoted side to play a strict defensive game in order to consolidate their position. But attacking football is our game, and it's not hard to understand why with fellows like Alan Woodward, Stewart Scullion, Geoff Salmons and Billy Dearden in the side. Manager John Harris's approach has always been open, ambitious soccer and we would not want it otherwise. Moreover, this outlook took the top clubs by surprise. Many people have asked me why promoted clubs usually find life at the top an arduous struggle. My answer is that so often clubs lack a sufficiently strong first time pool or just are not confident enough."

Currie's form in United's first season back in the top flight was a revelation – orchestrating much of United's fine forward play, spraying pinpoint 70-yard cross-field passes with either foot and chipping in with his fair share of goals, many of them spectacular long-range drives. In that opening period of games Currie had faced some of the finest midfield generals in the country and rather than being overawed, he had dominated. For United fans he was rapidly becoming the complete player.

With his tall, muscular build, trendy Dundreary mutton chops, long flaxen hair (once described by a female journalist as, "The Thatched Barn Look", much to Tony's chagrin), rock star looks and effortless style, his shirt worn raffishly outside his shorts, Currie was a natural pin-up, earning him adulation that hadn't been lavished on a Sheffield United player since the halcyon days of Jimmy Hagan. The fans to whom he waved and blew those trademark kisses even took to hanging around his home in Bishopscourt Road in Sheffield hoping to catch a glimpse of him; others wrote into Bramall Lane requesting locks of his hair; while the Bramall Lane terraces sang that his blue eyes shone like diamonds, that he walked on water and that he was the king of the land.

Praise for Currie was far from partisan, however. Such was Currie's impact on the First Division at the start of the 1971-72 season that the country's sports writers were soon clamouring for an England call-up for the young midfielder.

Even opponents were soon doffing their caps. "When we played against Sheffield near the start of the season

Currie really impressed me," Arsenal's vastly experienced double-winning skipper Frank McLintock told *Goal* magazine, showing a tremendous generosity of spirit – Tony had arrogantly 'megged him during their 24th August encounter.

After facing Sheffield's boy wonder twice more in the League Cup fourth round (in which the Blades emerged 2-0 replay victors after a hard fought goalless draw at Highbury), the Arsenal skipper was well qualified to offer his opinion: "This boy has all the skills – and power as well and he has that touch of arrogance that nearly all the class players seem to possess. He's a great prospect. I'm still trying to work out he managed to put a cheeky back heel flick through my legs inside the six-yard box during our first game this season."

The League Cup replay win against Arsenal on 7th October, however, highlighted not only the paucity of cover in United's ranks, but also the importance Harris placed on Currie.

It also offers further rebuke to those who regarded Currie as a dilettante.

Prior to the match while boiling an egg, Tony accidentally tipped the pan of scalding water over his right foot. It ballooned and blistered and he limped to the phone box (he didn't have one at home) to inform John Harris. Less than 24 hours later, Currie was remarkably passed "fit" to play his part in United's 2-0 win.

"I had four pain-killing injections before and during the match," Currie elaborates, "and although it deadened much of the pain during the match, afterwards it was absolute agony."

When interviewed in 1993, Tony revealed that it was, in fact, rare that he ever started a match in 100% condition: "[Injuries] were part of the game. It was bloody special to play and, if I played when not fully fit, it was usually my own fault."

At the start of October 1971, after ten undefeated games United (who had fielded the same starting XI throughout) were implausibly, but deservedly, top of the First Division.

It was, however, perhaps inevitable that it couldn't last and, sure enough, the run came to an end in their eleventh league game of the season against their nearest challengers at that time, Manchester United, at a sun-baked Old Trafford.

In front of 51,388 spectators an evenly contested encounter remained goalless until the 83rd minute when George Best decided to take on the Blades' defence single-handedly – waltzing past Trevor Hockey, Geoff Salmons and Gil Reece before squeezing in a right-footed finish of immortal quality from the tightest of angles. A second goal by Alan Gowling put the match beyond the Blades and condemned them to their first defeat since March.

Most pundits and the United players themselves believed the Blades had deserved at least a point: "If you saw the edited version of this match on Saturday night," wrote one journo, "you would be tricked into thinking that Manchester United were the best side and that is the greatest misrepresentation of the truth since Lord Haw-Haw."

"We got beat 2-0 at Manchester United," recalls Len Badger, "but the scoreline doesn't tell the whole story because we played quite well and could have been a couple of goals up. But Ted Hemsley got injured and that contributed to the special goal scored by George Best, which is regularly shown on TV. Gil Reece came on and played at left-back. Bestie picked the ball up and Gil stayed too close to Trevor Hockey. If Ted had been playing he wouldn't have done that; he'd have stayed off and forced him wide…Gil hadn't a clue what to do… he was a winger not a defender."

United's unbeaten run of league games had stretched to 21 matches. Not since the game against QPR in March had a league side so much as taken the lead against United, let alone beaten them.

The defeat at Old Trafford, however, was followed by a run of three more defeats, knocking United off the top of the league, before a 1-1 draw at home to Liverpool in October stopped the rot.

The Liverpool game found Currie in irresistible form and it was his unstoppable 40-yard pile driver that flashed past a helpless Ray Clemence to put United in front.

It was, without doubt, one of the best goals Currie had ever scored and prompted Kenneth Wolstenholme to exclaim on *Match of the Day*, "You'd have to through a whole season before you see a better goal than that!"

"[It was] like hitting a perfect golf shot," Currie reminisces. "I knew straight away it was going in because I caught the ball just right and it went like a rocket!"

Although Bill Shankly once allegedly wagered that Tony lived in a bungalow, as, in the Liverpool manager's opinion, "He'd nae want to be bothered with all that climbing stairs," in actual fact the Liverpool manager was a confirmed Currie devotee, and was particularly impressed by the player's work-rate.

"Not only is he big and strong and brave," Shankly commented after his side's draw at Bramall Lane, "he's clever as well. He can be very elusive. If he keeps on working as he is I have no doubt he will be an international player. He gets through a tremendous amount of running and he doesn't dawdle."

After the Liverpool result, Currie and United soon found themselves back in the groove, winning three of their next four games – including a 7-0 demolition of Bobby Robson's Ipswich Town.

Unfortunately, the Blades were unable to fully rediscover the momentum that had taken them to the top of the league and although they continued to serve up some scintillating football, inconsistency and a vulnerability to surprise defeats would dog them throughout the remainder of the season.

There were several reasons for this. Firstly, when injuries occurred, United's miniscule first team squad had insufficient strength in depth to cope.

"At the start of the season," Currie pointed out, "the same eleven players were going out there week-in, week-out but once we started picking up injuries, our results dipped."

Furthermore their emphasis on attacking play frequently left the Blades vulnerable to the counter attack sucker punch and, with gaps being left at the back, occasionally a good hiding.

In addition, as the season wore on teams wised up to their attack-minded tactics and were soon setting their stall out to suffocate United, and their danger man, Currie, in particular.

"We have certainly found [our emphasis on attack] to our disadvantage in home matches where visiting sides come first and foremost to defend," Currie observed. "In most games we were confronted by eight- or nine-man defensive barriers and as the season wore on it stifled our progress."

Four humiliations followed in quick succession. A five-goal mauling suffered in November at the hands of West Ham in the League Cup quarter-final, was followed by a

5-1 reverse at Crystal Palace in the first week of December, and worst of all, a 3-1 defeat to Cardiff City in the FA Cup.

As far as Tony was concerned the Cardiff game marked the turning point in United's season: "The biggest dent in our pride came in January," Currie recollected, "when lowly Cardiff convincingly knocked us out of the FA Cup in a third round tie before our own supporters. Although we kept plugging away our game deteriorated as the match progressed. But [Cardiff] played very well and on the day thoroughly deserved their win.

"From the ruins of that match, the club hit a depressing period when one poor performance followed another. We lost all our confidence and flair, matters reaching a climax with a 5-0 drubbing by Arsenal at home. Incredibly enough, in the early stages of the match we could have twice taken the lead but Bob Wilson pulled off a couple of breathtaking saves and before we knew where we were Arsenal were 2-0 ahead. In the second half they ran riot with Alan Ball pulling out all the stops."

It was during the Arsenal game that January that Ball famously sat on the ball in front of the main stand and contemptuously gestured for the United players to come and take it off him.

Tony remembers the incident well: "When Arsenal had absolutely stuffed us 5-0 at the Lane in 1972, Alan Ball just stopped and sat on the ball when I went to challenge him. Bally and I were good pals. I could have gone and kicked the ball from under him or whatever, but I didn't. I just stood there and clapped."

Currie nevertheless filed away the slight for future reference.

Tony concedes that his own form suffered during this period, a slump that was at least partially precipitated by the circulation, in February 1972, of malicious and unfounded rumours that he and goalkeeper John Hope had been consorting with loose women and indulging in late-night drinking sessions.

Although the smears were nothing more than idle gossip and were rightly dismissed as such by manager John Harris, they did, briefly, nevertheless have a detrimental effect on Currie both on and off the pitch.

Currie, who described himself as being "sickened and shaken for some weeks" by these malicious tall tales told the *Daily Express*: "I'm scared to make a mistake on the field because the crowd will believe more rumours. I've heard stories that my wife Linda has refused to let me in the house at night and I've slept outside in the car. It just isn't true."

On 8th February United had entertained Dynamo Kiev in a friendly at Bramall Lane. During the first half of a game in which United were outclassed (the Russians won 2-1), Currie let his frustrations get the better of him in the most uncharacteristic fashion.

Receiving the ball at one point during the first half Currie advanced to the edge of the Kiev penalty area, attempted to cut inside, lost control of the ball and in a fit of pique smashed it against the advertising hoardings. When the rebound came he thumped the ball again – this time into the crowd.

"I'm sorry I did this and I'd like to say so now," he pleaded for forgiveness in the following day's edition of *The Sheffield Star*. "I didn't mean to kick it into the crowd. I was fed up at having run the ball out of play, something no-one does deliberately. My action was foolish and I would like to apologise to the fans. I believe the ball struck the ball boy and I would like to say how much I regret this. If it is possible I would like the chance to tell him personally."

Although Tony's contrition was heartfelt and genuine it was evident that the rumours affecting his game would have to be dealt with, and, on 11th February, ahead of United's game at home to Manchester City the following day, Currie moved to nip them in the bud once and for all.

"John and I are fed up with these vicious stories concerning our personal lives," Tony told *The Sheffield Star*, "and there is no doubt that they have been affecting our games – and upsetting my wife, Linda. There is no truth in them, and I wish the people who start these ridiculous stories would get off our backs."

In many ways, Currie was a victim of perception. Just as his introverted character off the field could be mistaken for aloofness, his extravagant on-field showboating and appearance led some observers to label him a playboy.

In reality, Currie was a happily married family man with two young children – Sharon (born in 1969) and Ryan (born in 1971) – and has always scoffed at the notion that he was some sort of gadabout. "Because of the way I played people assumed I was a nightclubber," Currie later reflected, "which was never the case. On a Saturday night I used to take the wife out with all the other players and their wives, and at that time most of the squad would go out for a drink on a Monday night if we didn't have a midweek game."

Currie's appeal to the fans evidently worked and he and Hope were both given rousing receptions prior to the Manchester City match.

To repay the fans' belief, Currie vowed to rediscover his best form, opting for a simple remedy: "I realised the only way to regain my form was to fight all the harder with total concentration and determination. Thank goodness everything turned out all right in the end and I seemed to recover all my old zest in the game against Manchester

City, a throbbing 3-3 contest in which I scored with a powerful header from an Alan Woodward corner. Since then I haven't looked back."

Having fought his way back to his best Tony was selected by Alf Ramsey to play for the Football League in their annual inter-league fixture against the Scottish League at Middlesbrough's Ayresome Park on 15th March.

Although the fixture was declining in prestige and importance by 1972 (it would be phased out altogether in 1976), Ramsey still selected a strong side that included World Cup winners Bobby Moore and Geoff Hurst, Liverpool duo Ray Clemence and Emlyn Hughes and Newcastle centre-forward Malcolm Macdonald.

Currie made the most of his opportunity to further his case for inclusion in the full England set-up, capping an effervescent display with two goals and a hand in the other scored by Manchester City's Mike Doyle in the Football League's 3-2 win. In fact, many of the sports writers present nominated Currie as the man of the match.

"I was very pleased. I thought he had a fine game and was effective throughout," asserted John Harris who had made the trip to Middlesbrough to watch the match. "His goals were well taken and he deserved more."

Currie was delighted to be back to his best after the traumas earlier in the year.

"There was no doubt our confidence was shattered at that time," Tony confided to *The Green 'Un*, "and the appeal seems to have done a lot of good. People have been much more kind since and this has helped us. Life has been a lot better and now I'm happy we can put the cap on things by helping United get into Europe. We have a tough programme ahead but I'm sure we can do it. It was good to score the goals for the League team and I was disappointed I couldn't get the hat-trick. Maybe I was trying too hard."

Unfortunately, Currie's hopes of helping United push for a place in the UEFA Cup were dashed when injury ruled him out of action for four games (*and* kept him out of England's crunch European Championship quarter-final match against West Germany in April). The Chelsea fixture on 29th March 1972 was the first United league game Currie had missed since 26th December 1968 – a run of 136 consecutive league games!

Although United had fallen away in the second half of the season, with only four wins from their final 19 league games, to finish tenth in the league, their adventurous brand of play was deemed a breath of fresh air amidst a First Division populated by so many defensively-minded clubs. Although their brave convictions were occasionally punished when least expected, John Harris and his players never wavered from their belief in positive football, winning them many friends and admirers and a reputation as one of the most exciting teams in the country.

"Skill-wise we always knew we could do well," Tony Currie explains. "I'm sure clubs expected us to play defensively and we took them by surprise. Of course, the defeats made us feel sick at the time, but we realised that they had nothing to do with the way we should play. I hope we may have started an attacking trend."

"Everyone worked so hard," the late Trevor Hockey told *Goal* magazine. "We believed in ourselves and were always full of confidence. We played attacking football at home and away and built up a fantastic work-rate so that, instead of being overawed by the big names of the First Division we were showing them a thing or two."

It says much for the Sheffield United side that the players were disappointed merely to have finished in the top half of the table. "We'd have taken tenth place at the start of the season," Currie later recalled, "but to be at the top of the league for a couple of months and then finish tenth was a bit sickening really."

Certainly there was no shortage of ambition within the ranks. "I'm convinced the club is geared to be one of the most successful sides in the seventies," Currie announced in a contemporaneous interview. "The club has the enthusiasm to back such a drive. No one will be satisfied until we pick up a cup or two or get into Europe."

Overall, Currie was delighted with his contribution to United's season (which had seen him score eleven goals in all competitions) and was convinced that his first full campaign in the First Division had made him a far better footballer. "You have more time to use your skills and a player is allowed to express his natural talents," he reflected. "It has given me more experience and another important thing is you are able to learn something new in every match. In the Second Division the marking was so much tighter and defenders did not concede an inch of space."

Currie's reward for his self-assured form throughout the season was a first full England cap and a first appearance at Wembley – in the end-of-season Home International Championship fixture against Northern Ireland on 23rd May – a game that marked the first time since 1966 that England had started a match without a single member of their World Cup Final winning team.

Currie would later admit that his excitement about his first international call-up was tinged with apprehension: "I remember how nervous I was when I first got called up. There were people like Bobby Moore and Alan Ball in the squad – absolute legends – and I was worried about even checking into the hotel or walking into a room when they were there. But they took me under their wing and I came back feeling much more confident about myself and in my ability."

Sadly for Currie, the fulfilment of a life long ambition was marred by his substitution on 58 minutes, and ultimately, Ireland's first win – courtesy of a goal from Terry Neill (who had eluded his marker, Currie, to tap home following a Danny Hogan corner) – against the Three Lions since 1957. Remarkably, the Irish achieved their shock win without the help of George Best, who that week had announced the first of his many retirements from the game.

"I was called off after an hour and replaced by Martin Peters," Currie later recalled of his England debut. "Martin was, of course, much more experienced and Sir Alf Ramsey hoped he might be able to find a way through the packed Irish defence where a new boy couldn't. My old pal Malcolm Macdonald suffered the same fate ten minutes later when he was replaced by Martin Chivers, so we had a good old grumble together in the dressing room."

"I felt I did all right," Currie stated shortly after the game, in which, wearing the number 11 shirt, he had been played out of position on the left-hand side of England's midfield, "considering it was my first game for England and my first match at Wembley. Just thinking about the occasion took a great deal out of me. When I was taken off Alf Ramsey told me not to feel too badly. He said he'd done it to plenty of other internationals and they'd always had another chance."

Although Currie would have to wait until June 1973 for that next chance, six more Under-23 caps in the interim reassured him that he *was* very much in Ramsey's thoughts. Indeed Currie would have a large part to play in England's quest to qualify for the 1974 World Cup finals in Germany.

4

1972–74

"I should have had that tackle. I should have
put their fella and the ball into the Royal
Box. And then Shilts should have thrown his
cap on it. But these things happen, you don't
make mistakes on purpose."

– Norman Hunter

ALTHOUGH the admiration and kudos the club garnered throughout the 1971-72 season could hardly be displayed in the Sheffield United trophy cabinet, there was tangible reward for their attacking football in the shape of an invitation to participate again in the televised pre-season Watney Cup.

After a 3-0 win against Notts County (thanks to a goal from Woodward and two from Currie), Sheffield United were handed a semi-final date with Peterborough at London Road.

Despite having been reduced to ten men after 26 minutes when Tony Currie was sent off by referee Clive Thomas for a foul on Peterborough's Tommy Robson,

United cruised into the final with a comprehensive 4-0 victory. However, despite the introduction of automatic suspensions for sendings off, Currie's ban would not, in actual fact, commence until the start of the league season and he was therefore free to play in the final against Bristol Rovers who'd seen off Burnley in their semi.

Despite the presence of the television cameras and an impressive crowd of almost 20,000 at Rovers' Eastville stadium, the final disappointingly ended up goalless.

This meant that the 1972 Watney Cup Final, like the previous two finals (in which Manchester United and Colchester United had prevailed against Hull City and West Bromwich Albion respectively) would have to be decided on penalties.

Although United's first six penalties – taken by Woodward, Keith Eddy, Currie (scoring at the second time of asking, after the Rovers keeper was adjudged to have moved too early when saving his first effort), Billy Dearden, Eddie Colquhoun and Stewart Scullion (the latter in sudden death) were duly despatched, their Rovers counterparts matched them strike for strike. In the end United's hopes of winning the trophy were dashed when Ted Hemsley's effort was saved and consequently, United had lost 7-6 on penalties.

Despite losing out on a trophy, albeit a minor pot, there was compensation in the shape of new £50,000 signing Keith Eddy, whose successful penalty kick in the Watney final was his first touch as a United player. Tony was delighted to be reunited with yet another former Watford colleague: "Keith was a great player and I think if it hadn't been for Bobby Moore, he'd have played for England. He was such a good reader of the game and could pass a good ball. He was also calm and collected and a great penalty taker."

Less satisfactory was the exchange of Gil Reece (who was now 30) and Dave Powell (who had failed to recover sufficiently from the injury he'd picked up late in the promotion season), in addition to a small stipend, for Alan Warboys, the Cardiff City target man. Not only was it sad for Unitedites to see such popular figures move on but Warboys was not a success and six months later after only eight league and cup games (without a goal), United cut their losses and sold him on to Bristol Rovers.

Nevertheless Sheffield United had every reason to look forward to the new season with quiet optimism. Their first season back in the top flight had been negotiated with some panache, while the club's decision to build the South Stand was a massive morale booster to everyone connected with the club.

To proceed with the South Stand was, however, a massive gamble. The new stand, it was announced, would cost at least £650,000, and in bringing the rest of Bramall Lane up to the standard the club considered appropriate for a First Division side, the total expenditure on the ground was, reportedly, likely to be in the region of £1,250,000.

To generate the sums necessary to pay for it, vice-chairman Maurice Board went on record to say United would require league gates averaging at least 35,000 and nothing less than five seasons of league *and* cup success. Relegation, meanwhile, would amount to financial meltdown.

With Currie serving a three-match suspension following his Watney Cup indiscretion, United made a moderate start to the season, beating Birmingham away before losing two home games within the space of five days against Leeds and Newcastle. To add to United's woes Keith Eddy suffered a serious injury in the latter game that would rule him out until the New Year.

Currie's return against Stoke City on 23rd August (he would be ever present for the remainder of the season), inevitably saw a marked upturn in United's fortunes as the Blades embarked on a run which saw them lose just once out of 12 league and League Cup fixtures, and included impressive home wins against Chelsea, Manchester United and Arsenal.

The victory against Arsenal on 7th October, however, would prove to be United's last in the league for well over two months as the team went eight games without a win (a sequence that included six defeats), to fall from seventh to 17th place in the league table.

Although a win against Leicester City on 16th December stopped the rot, United ended the year with three more consecutive defeats. The last of those, a 4-1 hiding away at Newcastle on 30th December (during which Currie captained the side in the absence of Eddie Colquhoun), left United in a precarious 20th position just one point above the two relegation spots.

With Stewart Scullion and Geoff Salmons both having joined Keith Eddy on the long-term injuries list United's small squad had struggled to cope. It had been abundantly clear that reinforcements had been needed but, with £650,000 ring-fenced for the new stand, the transfer kitty was bare.

"Quite simply, it would be impossible to use this money for any other purpose," United chairman Dick Wragg stated peremptorily. "Our banks have agreed to advance us a certain sum of money to help us build a new stand. This sum has been specially negotiated for one purpose and one purpose alone."

If the United board were looking for a sustained cup run to bolster their financial *petard*, they would be sorely disappointed as United's failure to make any meaningful progress in cup football continued during the first half of the 1972-73 season. The Blades went out in the early stages of each of both the Texaco Cup (losing to West Brom) and the League Cup (losing at home to Arsenal).

With attendances declining rapidly at Bramall Lane as a result of the team's failings, the Sheffield United board members were purportedly close to panic. There were even rumblings that Harris would be moved upstairs again to make way for a younger, "tracksuit" manager.

Harris had never been an authoritarian taskmaster, trusting his players to exercise self-discipline off the pitch, and allowing them to express themselves on it. Deteriorating results were now calling this latitude into question, and the United board were worried about the temperament and character of their players, several of whom appeared to be suffering from an alarming loss of form. To compound this problem there was little or no money available to purchase reinforcements and the number of reserve players adequate for the high standards required in the First Division was lamentably low.

One of the areas of concern was that the previously solid midfield partnership of Trevor Hockey and Currie was no longer bossing games with the same authority that had previously made them such a potent force and, with Keith Eddy due to return from injury in the New Year, it was clear that one of them would have to make way.

While Currie's critics regarded his occasional dips in form as evidence of a lack of dedication and motivation, as far as Hockey was concerned Currie's inconsistency had more to do with the player's confidence: "He's got fabulous gifts," Hockey once opined, "but if he hit a bad pass he'd go off his game for a quarter of an hour. You had to kid him through a match. It was worth geeing him up because when he responded, we all benefited."

"I was always self-critical because I'm a bit of a perfectionist," Tony acknowledged, "so I could be moody if I didn't have a good game. I felt I did pretty well percentage-wise in the 600-odd games I played in my career. There were lots of times I was asked to play when I was probably only about 50-60 per cent fit and people didn't realise that."

In the event it was Hockey who was dropped to make way for Keith Eddy, and having lost his place, the Welsh international responded by handing in a transfer request. Although United could ill afford to drain yet more from their already shallow pool of players, his request was accepted and Hockey was on his way to Norwich City in an exchange deal that brought the Canaries' Scottish forward Jim Bone to Bramall Lane.

Although there were many who felt playing alongside Eddy always brought out the best in Currie, United's results remained maddeningly inconsistent in the New Year. Although the Blades went unbeaten throughout January to inch themselves away from the bottom two, they then went six games without a win, a run that saw them haplessly crash out of the FA Cup courtesy of an abject 2-1 defeat at Carlisle United.

Although a win away at relegation-threatened Crystal Palace on 13th March provided a temporary respite, four days later United were beaten 2-1 away at Everton during which Currie was sent off early in the second half for a bad challenge on John Connolly.

Oddly Currie wasn't suspended for his dismissal which meant he was free to remain ever present as United ripped up the form guide to finish the season in fine style. Courtesy of five wins and two draws from their remaining eight league fixtures (including a deserved win away at Old Trafford – a result which ruined Bobby Charlton's final appearance in front of his own fans), the Blades secured their immediate First Division future and a final League placing of 14th.

* * * * *

While Currie waited for his second full England cap, Alf Ramsey appointed him captain of his Under-23 side for the game against Wales at the Vetch Field on 29 November 1972. As the most capped player in the team that night (which included six players – Charlie George among them – winning their first Under-23 cap), Currie was the obvious choice.

"I enjoyed the responsibility of being skipper," Currie stated. "When Sir Alf asked me if I was prepared to accept the responsibility against Wales at Swansea I told him I would be delighted."

Winning his tenth Under-23 cap in the process, Currie led the team to a 3-0 win with all three goals coming in the first half courtesy of Malcolm Macdonald.

While Tony was honoured to be playing for and skippering the Under-23 side he was also understandably hungry and impatient for more full honours.

"Like most players," Currie acknowledged, "my main aim is to try and make the World Cup squad next season for the finals in Munich. That's obviously my biggest current ambition. I know there will be a tremendous challenge for places next season, but I'm hoping that my club performances will be good enough to help me claim a place in the squad."

After winning the last of his 13 Under-23 caps in the 1-0 win against Czechoslovakia in March 1973, Currie was handed his chance to stake that claim for Munich when he was included in the party for England's end-of-season summer tour, encompassing, over the course of an 18-day period, a friendly with Czechoslovakia in Prague, the crucial World Cup qualifier against Poland in Chorzow, and friendlies against the Soviet Union in Moscow and Italy in Turin. Tony would later describe his selection for the touring party as "one of the big moments of my career."

Although he missed the games against Czechoslovakia and Poland, when Alan Ball was sent off in the latter fixture for grabbing an opponent by the throat 12 minutes from the end of England's calamitous 2-0 defeat (which had placed England's participation in the 1974 World Cup in serious jeopardy) and because Colin Bell had to fly home because his wife had been taken ill, Tony was gifted a starting berth for the remaining two matches of the tour.

It was the opportunity Currie had been waiting for and he was determined not to waste it, performing admirably in England's 2-1 win against the Soviet Union in Moscow's Lenin Stadium.

"Currie in particular," purred *The Times*, "gaining only his second cap, adorned the midfield at times with unexpected and penetrating angles, an individual within a machine, lazy in movement, yet sardonically acute in style – a valuable acquisition..."

Four days later Tony kept his place in England's 2-0 defeat against Italy played in the sweltering heat of Turin – the first time England had been beaten by the Italians in 40 years and nine meetings. Currie, though, despite suffering from blistered feet, performed well, holding his own against the vaunted likes of Fabio Capello, Gianni Rivera and, in particular, the tough-tackling Romeo Benetti.

"I can remember playing against Romeo Benetti," Tony would wince in 2008. "He was the toughest player I ever came up against. I ended up having to give as good as I got and that was some challenge. Actually I quite enjoyed it."

Certainly the correspondent for *The Times* was impressed, singling Currie out for praise and complimenting his "moments of lazy Brazilian quality."

Almost overnight, Currie was widely being touted in the press (*The Times'* pejorative use, twice, of the "L-word" notwithstanding) as the saviour of England's midfield, which had for so long lacked the sort of creativity and guile that he could provide, and many even compared him to the man who had terrorised Alf Ramsey's England in the 1972 European Championship quarter-finals, Günter Netzer.

"Like the famous German midfield maestro," eulogised *Goal* magazine, "Currie sports a shock of blond hair, an in-born talent for conjuring up something different and an insatiable appetite for work in the engine room of the field. As the midfield guiding light behind most Sheffield United moves, the young England Under-23 skipper has much to command the comparison. Like Netzer he has strong legs, thick thighs and the priceless ability to find colleagues near and far with the chip or the bowed long field pass."

Currie was flattered by, enjoyed and recognised the comparison, although he has always stressed it was never one he ever cultivated intentionally: "Watching him play was like watching myself. He looked like me, he had the same hair as me and he played the same sort of way as me, although he was a bit more direct in that he would play it and go whereas I tended to spray my passes. But I didn't model myself on him any more than he modelled himself on me."

"Basically our styles are entirely different," Currie remarked on another occasion. "I mean a team is geared to his talents and he is obviously a great player. But I think

I am more of a team player and not such an individualist." Certainly the England national team would never be geared to the talents of Tony Currie, which is a travesty discussed elsewhere, and although Tony wasn't to know it at the time, his run of five games in 1973 would be his best ever run in the England side.

* * * * *

By the time Currie returned from England duty, the cricket era at Bramall Lane was drawing inexorably to stumps.

From a strictly playing point of view Currie was not entirely sure that the move to convert Bramall Lane to a four-sided ground would be beneficial to Sheffield United. "I'm sure [the three-sided ground] put other teams off," he later reasoned. "Gil Reece and Geoff Salmons used to love playing 'on the far side' with no-one in the crowd yelling at them to 'get on your wing!'"

Nevertheless, when the three-day Yorkshire versus Lancashire match ended in a rain-affected draw on 7th August, it went down in the annals as the last cricket match ever staged at Bramall Lane.

With the construction of the new South Stand about to begin, the Sheffield United board believed their priority was to finance the stand (funded largely by a £600,000 bank loan, repayable over five years) rather than the team. It would be imperative, therefore, that the entire first team squad remain fit throughout the 1973-74 season.

In the summer of 1973, pop band Limmie and the Family Cookin' released their catchy single 'You Can Do Magic', a tune which was soon adopted by the Bramall Lane faithful as a tribute to Tony Currie.

When the 1973-74 season started, Currie, buoyed by his return to the England team, set about underlining the aptness of his new theme tune with a vengeance, helping United to a 2-1 away win against Chelsea on 1st September, running Ron "Chopper" Harris ragged and sealing the victory with a glorious long range strike.

"He is the ideal midfield player," Harris doffed, "his strengths are his confidence, control and non-stop work-rate and he is very difficult to tackle in full flight… I think he must play for England."

As if to ram home the point, Currie was in imperious form three days later against Arsenal, a fixture that offered Tony the perfect opportunity to prove his worth against the man he'd replaced in the England team – Alan Ball.

Although they were rivals on the pitch, off it the two men were great friends, and Currie was deeply saddened by the World Cup winner's death in 2007: "We got on well. When I came into the England squad he took me under his wing, looked after me and made sure I was all right. That was a nice touch. He was the first person that you'd want sat next to you on a dinner table."

Having been trounced 5-0 by the Gunners the previous year, United's revenge was secured in the sweetest possible way. After 17 minutes, United were leading by four goals to nil and were cruising towards a famous 5-0 victory.

Currie (who netted two of the five goals – one a sweet 25-yard volley) could not resist showing Alan Ball he had not forgotten the World Cup winner's insult from the previous season, and famously sat on the ball – albeit with almost farcical consequences.

"We were leading 4-0," Currie recalled, "so it was just my chance to get my own back. The thing is that he did it on the halfway line and I did it in our box. When I got up, I tripped over the ball and they nearly scored from it! Bally came up to me after the match and said, 'Nice one, I'll have one for you next time.' He did because next time we played he put his foot on the ball and pretended to tie his laces. You wouldn't get away with this sort of antics nowadays."

That footballers were a less scrofulous breed in Currie's day hardly needs to be stressed but the following vignette from *The Sheffield Star* pleasingly belabours the point: "The night after United beat Arsenal 5-0 at Bramall Lane in September 1973 and Currie had done his famous sitting on the ball act with Alan Ball, we went out to see him. 'See if Currie will sit on the ball for us,' was the request. Not many names would have done it for nothing. Currie did it without demur."

Today a cadre of unctuous ten percenters would be selling exclusives to the highest bidder.

Whether Sir Alf Ramsey was impressed by or looked askance at Currie's latest monkeyshines is sadly unrecorded but either way Tony kept his place in the England starting XI for the friendly against Austria three weeks later.

Currie's performance in England's rampant 7-0 demolition of their opposition that night more than justified the manager's faith. In fact, Currie was at the heart of the rout, having a hand in several of the goals and capping a hugely accomplished display with his first goal for his country.

"I will always remember the moment I scored my first goal in an England shirt," Currie wrote in 1974. "It was on September 26th 1973, against a rather poor Austrian team. Although we ran out easy winners by seven goals to nil it was an exciting moment for yours truly. We were 5-0 up when Norman Hunter swung over an inch-perfect cross from the left wing straight to Martin Peters. The Tottenham midfield star headed the ball down to me, just outside the penalty area, and I met it perfectly on the volley and it flashed past the Austrian keeper."

England's win was the perfect confidence booster ahead of their crucial showdown with Poland the following month; and cause for the widespread belief that England would not only wipe the floor with the Poles but head to Munich as one of the favourites. The Austrian manager, Leopold Stastny, certainly thought so: "England can still teach the world how to play," he stated during his post-match interview. "On the evidence of tonight's performance, England will be in Germany and strong contenders for the World Cup."

But first England had to beat Poland at Wembley. The Poles had beaten Wales 3-0 in September and therefore only needed a draw to top the group and qualify. For England, however, only a win would do. Anything less would see England miss out on a place at the World Cup finals for the first time (England didn't deign to enter the first three tournaments). Such an outcome was unthinkable.

Over the years an urban myth has attached itself to the England versus Poland match of 17th October 1973: namely that England created chance after gilt-edged chance that time and again the Polish goalkeeper, Jan Tomaszewski, repelled with an inspired display of credulity-defying saves, some breathtaking, others wildly unorthodox.

There is a grain of truth in the myth, but a myth it sadly remains. While England did lay siege to the Polish goal from the second the referee blew his whistle, launching attack after attack, for the most part genuine penetration eluded them.

Indeed, most of the chances they contrived to create for the majority of the game were either snatched at, blazed high, wide or handsome, blocked by a wall of obdurate Polish defenders (and, on at least a few occasions, by

England's strikers making identical runs), or simply fluffed.

Tomaszewksi, meanwhile, didn't have a real save to make until the 37th minute, when he did well to push Colin Bell's firmly struck goal-bound drive round the post for a corner. Although the Polish keeper was twice more called into action during the remainder of the half – pushing a soft Allan Clarke header round the post and tipping a Mick Channon header over the bar – Tomaszewksi made both these saves look a great deal more spectacular than their actual threat merited.

As such, it was this irritating penchant for making a meal out of even the most routine of saves, coupled with his time-wasting, preference for punching the ball rather than catching it, and the fact that his defenders took his goalkicks, that famously inspired Brian Clough to describe Tomaszewski as a clown during the half-time interval.

England took to the field for the second half and picked up from where they had left off, but once again found themselves unable to break the deadlock. England's best chance at the start of the second half fell to Currie. After 52 minutes he was put clean through by Martin Chivers but with only the keeper to beat Currie slipped on the greasy Wembley surface and his left-foot shot sailed wide.

Five minutes later disaster struck.

When Currie failed to beat Polish left-back Adam Musial, the full-back came away with the ball and rolled an innocuous-looking pass up the touchline. When the ball reached the halfway line Norman Hunter seemed certain to reach it before the half-heartedly onrushing Gadocha and snuff out what little danger existed, either with a routine tackle or, failing that, a safety first hoof into the stands. Instead, Hunter meekly failed to live up to his "Bites Yer Legs" moniker when it mattered most.

"[Gadocha] came across," Hunter recalled in his autobiography, "and I remember thinking that the race for the ball would be a fifty-fifty situation but he slowed up. I had set myself for the tackle, thinking he would keep on coming. Unfortunately the ball went under my foot and he was off and away while I chased back, praying he wouldn't score."

Emerging with the ball following Hunter's botched challenge (a mistake which Hunter astonishingly repeated a few moments later when faced with the same player in virtually the same position on the park!), Gadocha advanced at pace before switching the play to the unmarked Domarski who bore down on England's exposed goalmouth.

"Gadocha played the ball forward to Anton Domarski and alarm bells started clanging in my brain," Peter Shilton recalls. "I came out of my goal to narrow the angle but at the very moment that Domarski let fly, I was momentarily unsighted by Emlyn Hughes, who had raced back to offer cover. It was vital that I saw Domarski's striking foot make contact with the ball so I could gauge its speed and trajectory and act accordingly. In that split second, my sight of him was blocked unwittingly by Emlyn Hughes. The Wembley pitch was very greasy, the ball skidded under my body and I knew from the position I had taken that it was goalbound."

It was.

"[Domarski] struck the ball well," Shilts continues. "It wasn't an easy shot to deal with because the Wembley Cumberland turf was springy and lush, which, on a wet night such as this, made the ball very greasy. When the ball hit the turf it came off lightning fast... what I should have done was make a blocking save, or parry the shot away for a corner. But I tried to get hold of the ball by scooping it into my body and retaining possession. It was the speed of the ball coming off the turf, together with the fact that I had been momentarily unsighted when Domarski actually struck it that beat me."

Wembley fell silent. England now needed two goals in the final half-hour of the match.

A minute later England appeared to have scored one of them when Martin Peters nodded a long throw-in from Chivers into the path of Mick Channon who side-footed nonchalantly into the net. Unfortunately for the home side, the Belgian referee had spotted Peters climbing all over a Polish defender and the goal was chalked off.

England did not have to wait too long for a legitimate equaliser when Martin Peters was bundled over on the edge of the area, as he was about to break through. It was a clear penalty and in the face of extreme pressure Allan Clarke coolly sent Tomaszewski the wrong way to level the scores.

England continued to bombard the Polish goal, now with increased desperation and with roughly ten minutes to go Tomaszewski made his second (and last) breath-taking save of the evening. When the ball fell to Allan Clarke in the six-yard box, the Leeds striker was given what seemed like an age to pick his spot. It seemed certain that the man they nicknamed Sniffer would score but Tomaszewski athletically saved his half-volley at point-blank range. It was a save worthy of the best and was as sure a sign as any that it was not going to be England's night.

On the touchline, Ramsey still refused to make the changes the situation demanded, despite his increased agitation.

"He looked close to panic," recalled the late Bobby Moore (who watched the drama unfold from the substitutes' bench). "You could see... his bottle had gone. I kept urging him to make a substitution but he convinced himself that the men on the pitch could do it."

When Ramsey did finally make a change, bringing on Derby County's Kevin Hector in place of the ineffectual Chivers, barely 90 seconds remained on the clock.

And yet Hector almost won it with a header from an in-swinging Tony Currie corner. With Tomaszewski having gone on yet another walkabout and with the goal at his mercy, Hector's point-blank header could only find the midriff of the Polish defender on the line.

In injury time England had one final chance to win it but once again Colin Bell's goalbound effort was cleared off the line by a back-pedalling Polish defender. England's last chance had, like so many others, gone begging and seconds later the referee blew his whistle for the end of the game. The game had finished 1-1 and it was Poland and not England who qualified for Munich. The unthinkable had happened.

"Some of the lads were in tears," Currie recalls of the emotional aftermath, "and Sir Alf had a difficult time consoling them."

"The England dressing room was like a morgue," Peter Shilton agreed. "Everyone was totally drained and devastated… I have never known such a feeling of emptiness."

"We annihilated them but we simply couldn't put the ball in the net," Currie concluded later. "It was an accumulation of bad finishing, lucky goalkeeping and good goalkeeping – and fate."

From an individual perspective, Currie had played well, delivering a number of glorious crosses from the right wing and umpteen high quality corners as well as offering a number of long-distance efforts that had at least tested the Polish keeper.

Additionally Currie gave the ball away with less frequency than his midfield colleagues and rarely tried to over-elaborate like so many of his team-mates did on a greasy surface and against the sort of determined defending that made the prospects of dribbling past the massed Polish backline little more than a delusion. If Currie did miss a couple of chances, he had not been the only guilty party in this regard.

"We all sat in the dressing room afterwards and not a word was said," Currie recalls of the post-match devastation. "Everyone was in shock. I was walking around in a deep depression for months afterwards and I'm sure most of the others would tell you the same. As it panned out, I wouldn't have been able to play in the finals because of my cartilage, but for some of them it was their last chance. We didn't feel we let anybody down. It was just bad luck and you had to accept it. I think we would have caught some flak from the fans had we performed badly but we gave everything that night and they knew it. That was what kept the hounds off our backs. The press were quite good about it because they knew it too. It was like somebody boarding the bloody goal up. Having said that, I don't suppose it helped having Chivers, Channon and Clarke up front with no wide man. They were all very much the same sort of player, down the middle centre-forwards."

While England had undoubtedly dominated the match from start to finish and were left to rue a host of missed chances and two costly errors, the nation has collectively wiped from its memory the fact that the outcome of the Poland game could have been much worse. With roughly eight minutes to go McFarland had cynically and disgracefully wrestled Lato to the floor when the clinical striker (who won the golden boot at the following year's

World Cup finals, scoring seven goals) had effectively broken clean through on Shilton's goal. Nowadays, as "last man", McFarland would have been given a straight red card, but instead the Derby defender escaped with a yellow and stayed on the field. If anything, therefore, it had been Poland who were cheated that October night.

While the consequences of England's failure to win, the result, taken at face value and on its own merits, looks a fairly presentable one.

After all, England had played with an emphasis on attack rarely witnessed under Ramsey (and even less so these days) and had completely dominated a Polish side that in the following year's World Cup finals would beat Argentina, Haiti, Italy, Yugoslavia, Sweden and finally Brazil to win the third place play-off. Having also beaten England during qualification, it was clear that this Polish side were far from mugs. Certainly they deserved a great deal of credit for their tenacious refusal to capitulate to England's non-stop bombardment, soaking up everything Ramsey's men could throw at them in front of arguably the most vociferously partisan Wembley crowd since the 1966 World Cup Final.

While the press ultimately recognised that the players had tried the hearts out, they didn't have far to look for a scapegoat; namely, Sir Alf Ramsey. It was, in their opinion, the England manager's negative and cautious approach in the previous games, particularly in the draw against Wales, that had been as responsible for England's failure to qualify for the 1974 World Cup finals as the inability to beat Poland at Wembley.

Having failed to cultivate a fruitful relationship with the media during his reign, Ramsey was powerless to silence the swelling chorus of voices now calling for his head. Although Ramsey soldiered on for two more matches – a 1-0 friendly defeat against Italy at Wembley (in which Currie played, and in the opinion of *The Times* was, "the one man [in the English team] with a wide vision in midfield and creative instincts") and a 1-1 friendly draw with Portugal (which Currie missed through injury), Sir Alf was finally relieved of his duties at some nebulous date in April 1974 (the FA had given Ramsey eight grand to go on holiday, effectively ushering him out of the country and away from the press, before officially announcing his departure on 1st May).

With Ramsey's departure, Currie's international career effectively went with him. It soon became clear that Sir Alf's long-term replacement – Leeds boss Don Revie fresh from guiding his team to the Division One title for a second time – had no serious interest in selecting the fabulously gifted but mercurial players he had at his disposal. Heinously, over the course of his 29 matches in charge of the national team, Tony would win only one cap.

5

England Under Revie

"The new generation of playmakers –
Hudson, Currie, Bowles and Marsh – lived
dangerously, and often found themselves
marginalized. The skilled playmaker, who
at one point would take it upon himself to
entertain the crowd, had become a byword
for a 'lazy' player. It was not just these players
whose professionalism was questioned. Stylish
forwards with flair often found themselves
playing second fiddle to runners who could
trap a ball further than they could kick it."

– Jimmy Greaves

"[Don Revie] didn't exactly like us
too much so it was quite easy to have a
mutual feeling really."

– Tony Currie

"Unfortunately Revie took over and he got rid of all the flair players. And he struggled as a result because you need the top players. You have got to have the balance right – you can only have one or two in the side. But if you don't have them at all then you're going nowhere, as it proved with Don Revie."

— Frank Worthington

SOON after his appointment as England manager in July 1974 Don Revie gathered no fewer than 81 current and potential players for an overnight bonding session at a Manchester hotel. Naturally Currie was among them.

While it was undoubtedly an innovative experiment by Revie – designed perhaps to recreate the sense of unity and familial camaraderie that he had famously instilled at Leeds or to encourage the massed ranks of England's fringe players by suggesting that they were in the thoughts of the paterfamilias (although 47 of the invitees would never play for their country) – it was not one that any England manager has ever repeated.

In addition, not everyone was convinced by Revie's thinking, with some interpreting it as being an early indication of the new manager's indecisiveness. Certainly that was the view of Derby County central defender Colin Todd: "To invite so many to what was just a get-together was odd. I could understand Don wanting to get to know his squad, but to bring more than 80 along just suggested he had no idea who should be in the team."

One thing Revie did appear to be certain about however was that there would be little room in his plans for the so-called mavericks – Frank Worthington, Stan Bowles, Rodney Marsh, Alan Hudson, Peter Osgood and Charlie George – the group of supra-talented, unorthodox, game-changing individuals with whom Currie's name is commonly lumped; players for whom Revie's peremptory curfews, dossiers and the pre-match sessions of bingo and carpet bowls he'd hosted at Elland Road were never going to sit comfortably.

"I remember that the first thing he said to us [at the Piccadilly Hotel]," Frank Worthington recalls, "was that nobody was allowed to go out that night, which came as a bit of a shock."

"I think he was trying to wind us up," Alan Hudson believes, "so we'd walk out and he'd have an excuse [to get rid of us]."

Inevitably a number of the usual suspects – Worthington, Hudson, Alan Ball, and according to Hudson, Currie – decided to ignore Revie's orders and hit the town.

"We went to a couple of casinos," Worthington chuckles, "and I think we all eventually met up in George Best's club, Slack Alice's, later on in the night. When he found out about it the following day, I don't think Don Revie saw too kindly to the situation."

"So he pulled us aside," Hudson chips in, "and just said our attitude was terrible, which was nonsense really."

Although Hudson recalls Currie as being among the recalcitrants, Tony denies he was with them: "They all went out," Tony insists. "I wasn't one of them. Honest."

Whether Currie was among those quaffing champagne in the early hours in Manchester is actually neither here nor there, at least as far as the England manager was concerned. Revie had clearly already tarred him with the same brush as the rest of the bad lads and made his reservations known.

"[Revie] made it clear that players like myself, Stan Bowles, Alan Hudson, Rodney Marsh and Frank Worthington didn't figure in his plans," Currie recalled. "I suppose he thought we weren't team players."

"Don Revie took us to one side," Frank Worthington concurs, "I think it was Alan Hudson, Tony Currie, Stan Bowles and me and he made it quite plain to us that we were not his type of player."

Although Currie did start Revie's first unofficial game in charge – a match that saw an England XI play Sheffield Wednesday at Hillsborough on 21st October as part of the testimonial for the Owls' long-serving general manager Eric Taylor – and played his part in his side's comfortable 5-0 victory, there would be no place for him in Revie's line-up when England took on Czechoslovakia in a European Championship qualifier nine days later.

Although Currie did keep his place in the squad (alongside fellow mavericks Alan Hudson and Frank Worthington) for Revie's first official match, only the latter actually featured in the game (which ended in a not entirely convincing 3-0 England win).

Worthington, though, would make just one more England appearance (as a substitute in Revie's second match in charge), and while Hudson would make his debut in Revie's third match in charge, he would play his last match for England in Revie's fourth. Currie, and for that matter Stan Bowles and Charlie George, at least initially, were ignored by Revie completely.

Despite his non-selection of the country's most gifted individuals, Revie made a bright start to his reign with six wins and three draws from his first 365 days in charge.

And yet it wasn't that Revie was reluctant or unwilling to change a winning team, or at least a team that wasn't losing; in fact he was *always* tinkering with his selections, much to the disquiet of his boss, FA secretary Ted Croker.

"He was changing his mind all the time," Croker later criticised. "It changed my whole outlook on the sort of person who was a good England manager... Alf [Ramsey] judged a player by international appearances – after the previous game barring one or two injuries, he knew what his team was going to be for the next game. I think that is one of the most important features of a manager's success... he must not respond to the public clamour you tend to get to try this new lad or that new lad. You will always lose out. But Don was completely different. After an international match, he would come in and have a chat about who had played well and who had played badly, and I could see his thoughts about the team. Then he would watch a game the next week and see one of the players who had played well or badly, and be influenced by that, or he'd see another player who had played exceptionally well in a team doing well and be tempted to bring him in. There were constant changes going on. From that experience I recommended to his successors, Ron Greenwood and Bobby Robson, that the most important thing was to try and keep a settled team. You get player loyalty, too, that Don never really got at international level."

This was what was so baffling and remarkable about Revie's stewardship: "In ten years," Revie's biographer Andrew Mourant writes, "there had been more stability within Leeds United than at any other league club. It came as a surprise to almost everyone that one of Revie's characteristics during his England reign was a chronic inability to decide on his best team."

During Revie's first eight games in charge there did, however, seem to be a semblance of clear thinking regarding the midfield, where the manager's preferred choices were Manchester City's Colin Bell, Arsenal's Alan Ball and Queens Park Rangers' skipper Gerry Francis, each of whom were perhaps rather more celebrated for their athleticism and industry than their ability to conjure something out of nothing. But while it might be difficult to condemn Revie for placing those three in front of Currie in the queue it is somewhat less easy to rationalise his selections when any of these men were not available.

Certainly it must have hurt to see comparative journeymen such as Burnley's Martin Dobson, Manchester City's Dennis Tueart, and Ipswich's South African-born Colin Viljoen seemingly ahead of him in the queue.

Although Revie had selected Currie (and Hudson) in the All Star XI he put together to take on Joe Mercer's West Midlands XI in the benefit match for those injured or bereaved in the Birmingham bombings that was held at St Andrew's on 9 December 1974, it wasn't until the ninth game of his reign that Revie finally got around to recalling Currie to full England duty.

Just as Alan Ball's red card against Poland in 1973 had paved the way for Currie's second cap against the USSR, it was the surprising omission of the same player that opened the door for Currie to win his seventh, against Switzerland in Basle on 3rd September 1975.

Although Ball had skippered England in each of the previous six fixtures under Revie – which had included the impressive 2-0 win against West Germany, the 5-0 demolition of Cyprus and, most recently, the 5-1 rout of the Scots – because Ball had failed to set a captain's example by observing and enforcing a midnight curfew during a recent England get-together, the World Cup winner was not even called up for the squad!

To add insult to injury, Ball only discovered the news when a journalist seeking his reaction called his wife. At barely 30 years of age, and after ten years of impeccable service that encompassed two World Cups and 72 caps, Ball's international career was unexpectedly and prematurely over.

As far as Currie was concerned, his selection, in Ball's place, against the Swiss had more to do with pressure from the press than any desire on Don Revie's part. The England manager, Currie believes, still had grave concerns about his work-rate.

"Before the international against Switzerland in 1975," Currie recalls, "we held one of the first press conferences to include players. I'm up there in front of all these reporters and they start asking me about work-rate. The only reason they did that was because Revie had mentioned it to them. So, because I was influenced by what people said about me, I went out and ran my balls off... It affected my game."

England may have won that night in Basle but it was an uncomfortable evening which did little to silence the manager's growing band of critics. Although England scored twice in the first 18 minutes to open up a two-goal advantage through Keegan (who also missed a spot kick on 12 minutes) and Channon, following Switzerland's reducer on the half-hour it was all one-way traffic, which the overworked England back four did well to repel.

Currie may have run his wotsits off against the Swiss, in a bid to alter Revie's preconceived attitude towards him, but it had evidently not been enough. Revie never picked him again.

With a manager in charge who was greatly influenced by the opinions of the press, Currie's case was hardly helped by *The Times* reporter who offered the following coup de grace: "Currie [allowed] his feet to take him where his mind wanted to go...Bell, as usual [was] the workhorse."

"People say I played for myself – but that's rubbish," Tony contends. "I never did that although I reckon perhaps if I had played for myself more and not for the team... I might have impressed the boss and stayed in the side."

This seems unlikely. It was perspiration rather than inspiration, workhorses rather than thoroughbreds that were the foundations on which Revie built his England team.

Revie evidently believed that at international level it was acceptable for his players to lose the ball through ineptitude or a lack of technique, but if a player wasted possession through an ambitious use of skill, or allowed his "feet to take him where he wanted to go", that was deviating from sacrosanct tactical dogma. Perhaps Duncan McKenzie, who was never capped by England, put it best when he said: "The attitude in England is that tricks are OK if they work. If they don't, you're a w*****."

The player who perhaps best exemplified the Revie era was the diligent Kevin Keegan, a player who evidently ticked all of the manager's boxes, as Peter Shilton observes: "Flair in the England team was unfashionable. In the seventies, individualism often lost out to the team ethic. Those who played to the gallery found little favour. Don warmed to Kevin Keegan, he liked his work ethic. Kevin Keegan was not a flair player but he made the most of what he had. He knew he wasn't the best player in England at the time, but he was always working on it."

England's naturally talented, creative players didn't fit into the regimented way Revie ran the England team. Revie distrusted their individuality and their unorthodoxy, and couldn't trust them to stick to his rigid, preconceived game plans. "Perhaps that was why they never found favour with Don Revie," Shilton concludes, "who wanted his players to carry out his instructions to the letter."

Having failed to do himself justice against the Swiss, it probably did not therefore come as much of a surprise to Currie when he was left out of England's vital European Championship qualifier against Czechoslovakia the following month (along with four others who had started against Switzerland) which ended in a disastrous 2-1 defeat.

With England's hopes of making the quarter-finals hanging by a thread, nothing but a resounding win in their last fixture away in Portugal would steer them back on course. However, rather than sending for Currie or Hudson (who had been so instrumental in the victories over West Germany and Cyprus) to partner Gerry Francis, Revie instead turned to Trevor Brooking (whom he had dropped a year earlier) and Leeds United's primarily defensive utility man Paul Madeley.

It was yet another new-look midfield and yet another abject display, which resulted in a rather fortunate 1-1 draw that effectively ensured England's elimination from the tournament at the group stage.

England's draw in Lisbon left the Czechs in the box seat. Needing only a draw in Cyprus, the Czechs beat the Cypriots 3-0 to top the group and qualify ahead of England before famously going on to win the tournament, beating West Germany on penalties.

Having failed to guide England to the later stages of the European Championships, which was then, as now, the minimum requirement for an England manager, the anti-Revie lobby was steadily growing in number, conducted by an ever growing number of disillusioned England stars.

Alan Ball, still smarting from his unceremonious defenestration, was already waging tabloid war on England's beleaguered coach, while Emlyn Hughes and Alan Hudson also publicly criticised Revie.

Ball and Hughes, two fiercely patriotic men for whom the privilege of representing their country was payment enough, had been incensed by Revie's negotiation of increased draw and win bonuses in addition to their basic appearance fee.

Ball, furthermore, asserted that Revie was afraid of independent spirits within his camp and only selected yes men, while Hudson groused that Revie's idea of team building by playing bingo and carpet bowls could have been just as easily achieved by taking the team down the pub!

"Some of the players are donkeys," Ball pertinently scoffed. "Give them a lump of sugar and they run all day and play bingo all night."

Ball, Hughes and Hudson were not the only ones who were disillusioned. In the summer of 1976, goalkeepers Phil Parkes and Peter Shilton even went so far as to announce that they no longer wished to be considered for England (although Shilton later reversed his decision). Parkes had been insulted when Revie opted not to replace Ray Clemence at half-time against Wales in 1976 (despite telling the QPR keeper that he would play the second half); while Shilton was merely frustrated by the lack of opportunities now that Clemence was obviously Revie's first choice.

Even those who publicly remained silent had their doubts. Mick Channon, who won more caps than anyone else under Revie, believed the manager went overboard with tactics. "I don't think he needed to do that. Alf Ramsey simply said: 'This is what we're going to do... So and so take him.' We'd do a couple of little free-kick routines and that would be the end of the story. Eventually with Revie your mind was full of too much... you could end up a nervous wreck. Some would take the dossiers seriously, though to others they were a joke… Players aren't really that intelligent. They didn't need all that. They just want to play football."

While Currie also kept his counsel at the time, he too regarded Revie's coaching methods and dossiers hard to digest, later remarking with dry understatement, "Don Revie often used to fill his players' heads with useless information."

Revie it seemed was, nevertheless, prepared to give Currie one last chance, selecting him for the Inter-League fixture between the Football League and the Scottish League in March 1976 at Hampden (the last match of its kind). With a side that contained ten England internationals, a solitary Trevor Cherry goal won the match for the Football League. Currie, however, did not do enough to impress Revie (the *Scotsman* newspaper describing Currie and his team-mates Jimmy Greenhoff and Dennis Tueart as "failures") and when the squad was announced for the summer's Home Internationals and England's trip to America where they were due to play Brazil and Italy as part of the Bi-Centennial Tournament, Tony's name was not included in either.

Although Currie was convinced that a move to Leeds would enhance his international prospects, the start of the 1976-77 season saw Revie at last stumble upon a settled line-up with Pearson, Keegan and Channon up front and Trevors Cherry and Brooking and Gerry Francis in midfield.

But when this first choice axis was disrupted by injury there was still no route back for Currie even when Revie most needed his ingenuity.

In November 1976 England travelled to Rome for a World Cup qualifier against Italy that they literally could not afford to lose. Although Revie chose this match to recall Stan Bowles and Emlyn Hughes, Revie's midfield selections against the Italians were baffling – picking Trevor Cherry and Brian Greenhoff to play alongside Trevor Brooking.

In fielding *two* players who were both essentially central defenders in midfield roles, Revie left England without a prayer of navigating a way past the Italians' redoubtable back line.

Despite the presence of Bowles England utterly failed to threaten the Italian goal and Revie's men were generously flattered by their 2-0 defeat.

It was this result coupled with a failure to score heavily against the minnows of the qualifying group, Finland and Luxembourg, that ensured England would fail to qualify for a second World Cup in succession. Although England finished level on points and goals conceded with Italy it was the Azzurri who secured qualification as the group winners by virtue of having scored three more goals.

With 'Revie Must Go' headlines now dominating the back pages of the newspapers, Revie obliged his critics by deceitfully signing a £340,000 four-year contract to manage the United Arab Emirates' national side, leaving the FA to learn about his mendacity in the papers.

Although Revie's departure would ultimately benefit Currie to the tune of ten more England caps, Tony, like so many, was nevertheless disgusted but not surprised by Revie's disgraceful treachery.

"It didn't surprise me when he did that. It summed him up," Currie asserts. "The way he quit badly tarnished the image and reputation of our game. He just did not give any consideration to the effect it would have, but that was typical of the man. I found him to be a selfish person. He wanted to be close to the players but never achieved it because he treated us like schoolboys."

Currie remains understandably bitter to this day about his spell in the international wilderness: "People always talk about my work-rate, but that's a load of crap. I worked hard, but I'm sure my reputation didn't help me. Revie didn't like my style of playing. He played me once in three years. He capped 90-odd players in his time, but I had one chance against Switzerland in 1975 and that was it. End of story. I was in every squad of his, but I never got a look-in. People picked up on it. They'd say Currie is a weed or he doesn't tackle, so I'd go out, run my bollocks off and let it affect my game. I should have ignored it, but I couldn't. I hate it when people say I was lazy, because it wasn't true. I was a perfectionist. I wanted to be the greatest player to ever pass a ball.

"Managers always have their favourites and I obviously wasn't Revie's. People in this country always seem to want to find fault when you have talent. They see you play half a season and you're out of this world, but then they worry about the other half. What they fail to consider is that opposition are always trying to stop you. It was always 'Stop Currie' or 'Stop Hudson' and you stop their team playing. You might have two players on you throughout a match trying to kick you to bits, so whenever you get the ball you have no bloody time. But all people think is, 'Currie didn't want to play today.' That wasn't the case at all. People like me and [Charlie] George and Hudson wanted to play every week. We always wanted to be the best player on the field, to have our names in the headlines. People called me lazy and said I was an individual. I was a team player who blew kisses to the crowd."

During a period when England failed to qualify for the finals of a single major tournament, to say it was perverse that the country's most singular individuals were constantly overlooked for the national team, is surely something of an understatement. Would England have failed so consistently and so conspicuously under Revie had he regularly picked these men? Certainly Tony Currie doesn't think so.

"When we've been together we've often talked about it, you know the likes of Stan and Frank and Alan Hudson and so on," Currie stated, "that it would have been nice to have all played in the same team. I'm sure the other team would have struggled to get the ball off us."

"TC and I should have been automatics in bringing the English game back to its senses," Alan Hudson wholeheartedly concurs, "with the experienced Alan Ball in between us. That midfield would have been the backbone of English football for a very long time and would have been followed by the young and very classy Glenn Hoddle. Nowadays clubs have to import players with those sort of skills."

A better coach would surely have found a way of harnessing the idiosyncratic talents of Currie and Hudson *et al*, or better still, built a team around them. Instead Hudson and Worthington were only deemed worthy of two caps apiece during Revie's 29-game tenure, while Currie and Charlie George were only handed a desultory one each.

"It's when you look back that it hurts, more so now than ever," Tony reflects. "Why didn't I do this, why didn't I do that? Why didn't the England managers pick me more often? Why didn't they pick Worthington, Hudson, Bowles and Currie in the same team? Why didn't someone say, 'Right, I'm going to pick them all for three games and see how it goes?' I'd love to have seen somebody brave enough to do that. It just needed a brave man to pick us all.

"Unfortunately we didn't have that man."

6

1974–76

"Of course you're tempted when a big club like that comes in for you, but I didn't like change and I was very happy where I was. Perhaps I was wrong, maybe I should have gone to Manchester United and replaced Charlton."
– Tony Currie

MIDWAY through the 1973-74 season changes were afoot at Bramall Lane. Things had not been going well. Keith Eddy and young keeper Tom McAlister had both suffered serious injuries and an indifferent sequence of results found Sheffield United languishing in 14th position in the league table, just three points above the relegation zone.

In a bid to stop the rot, John Harris was again "moved upstairs" for a second spell as general manager, and on 7th December, 42-year-old Blackburn Rovers boss Ken Furphy – the man who had handed Currie his league debut at Watford – was appointed as manager of United's team affairs.

With the expensive ground developments in the offing, the new manager sought assurances from the board that he had not been hired as the patsy who would underwrite the South Stand by supervising the sale of United's most valuable assets. In fact, Furphy was reassured that the stand would pay for itself.

"They told me they'd got £250,000 in their account," Furphy explains, "a £500,000 deal with a supermarket behind one goal and a £250,000 deal with a petrol filling station on one corner…."

Catastrophically, six weeks after Furphy's appointment, the Sheffield City Council refused the necessary planning permission for the supermarket and United's development plan lay in tatters.

Despite such setbacks, and the apparent lack of any contingency plans, one thing was certain: the South Stand would not be part-financed by the sale of their biggest box-office draw, Currie, despite overtures from a variety of clubs, the most persistent of whom was Manchester United, whose manager Tommy Docherty wanted Tony to replace the soon-to-retire Bobby Charlton. In a blatant breach of procedure that would now be termed "tapping up," Old Trafford representatives even took to phoning Tony at his home!

In the face of this pursuit, it was only natural that Tony should at least contemplate a future away from Bramall Lane.

"I have to confess that I began to feel a bit restive," Tony conceded. "I was still ambitious, and although I was grateful for the fact that Sheffield United had given me the chance to hit the big-time, I felt that perhaps I might win honours more quickly with another, more fashionable club."

In order to nip any temptation in the bud, the Sheffield United board moved swiftly to secure Tony's long-term future. During contract negotiations with United's chairman Dick Wragg and John Harris, Currie received assurances that the board's ambitions matched his own and a pledge that the United team would be rebuilt around him.

"It took a bit of talking to sort things out," Currie explained, "but eventually I decided that all was not gold that glittered, and I agreed to sign a new contract for the Blades. It was clear that they had ambitious plans for the future themselves, and they convinced me that I was one of the key men in those plans."

Despite the boost Currie's international prospects and quest for domestic honours would have received from a move across the Pennines, Currie was content, as Docherty witheringly put it, to remain "a big fish in a small pond" and loyally put pen to paper on a new five-year contract (with the option of an additional year) designed to keep him at Bramall Lane until he was 30.

Despite his barbs, the Manchester United boss was gutted that his target had slipped through his fingers. "Paddy Crerand [Docherty's assistant] and I tried ever so hard to get Currie, and [Manchester] United were happy to pay the fee," 'The Doc' admitted many years later, "but Sheffield United wouldn't sell him. It was a real shame because he was tailor-made for Old Trafford."

Incidentally, when Tony signed his new contract with Sheffield United there was but one contractual rider: "A gentleman's agreement with the chairman saying I could move on if we got relegated."

It is worth noting that despite his worth to the club, both commercially and on the playing side, and the wages being waved in his direction from potential suitors, Currie never demanded or held out for more money at this or any other stage of his playing career.

"The contracts I signed were always the ones offered," Currie confirms. "I never knew you could hold out for more or extras or clauses. For me, a contract was offered and you signed them."

Nevertheless, even the fact that Currie had put pen to paper did not deter yet another club from sniffing around, this time Arsenal, who were reputed to be offering a fee of somewhere in the region of £300,000. Some Fleet Street wag even had Currie looking at houses in the North London area precisely one day after signing his new contract in South Yorkshire!

"I have had a bellyful of all this," chairman Dick Wragg raged. "The latest report about him leaving is a load of rubbish. Tony has got a new contract and is staying here. The rumours we have had unsettle players and I hope they now finish once and for all. Times without number I have stated that Sheffield United are interested in buying good players, not selling them."

* * * * *

As so often happens when a new manager comes in, United's league form initially picked up, losing just two of the ten league games that followed Furphy's appointment (although United crashed out of both domestic cup competitions during this period). Currie also seemed boosted by the arrival of the man who had given him his Watford debut, conjuring several moments of genius during this run: setting up two of Alan Woodward's hat-trick goals and scoring the fourth himself in the Blades' 4-2 home win against Southampton on 22nd December.

On Boxing Day, during the Blades' visit to Old Trafford, Currie was again at his flamboyant best, putting the visitors on their way to a 2-1 win with a goal at the Stretford End, after which he stood and blew kisses to the home fans he'd recently spurned and who had been goading him from the kick-off.

Three weeks later, during United's 2-1 away win at Burnley's Turf Moor, Currie conjured another piece of unforgettable brilliance scoring the winner with a stunning 25-yard half-volley.

Although a pulled thigh muscle (sustained during a County Cup match against Sheffield Wednesday on 26th January) forced him to miss the whole of February 1974 (during which United won only once), when he returned in March for the game against Manchester United, Currie was appointed United's skipper, replacing Eddie Colquhoun. Furphy, who once called Currie the greatest player in the world, was convinced that the additional responsibility would boost both Tony's morale and help his international prospects. "This chap has a treasure chest of talent," Furphy confided in a local journalist, "and so far he has scarcely opened the lid…"

"If a player grumbled to me about him disappearing from the game," Furphy would later expound, "I would simply tell him to give Tony the ball. The fact that he didn't go chasing around didn't bother me because I knew what he could do when he had the ball."

Unfortunately after only five more games, Currie's season (in which United finished only four points clear of relegation) was brought to a premature end when he returned from England's trip to Portugal at the start of April (on which he had once again warmed the bench throughout a goalless draw) in urgent need of a cartilage operation.

Remarkably Tony had been playing through an intense pain barrier for over a fortnight.

"My knee actually went when we played Manchester City away [on 16th March]," Tony explained. "It didn't happen in a tackle or anything like it. I think it'd been building up for a while. I'd had pain in the knee off and on for six months."

It was the first time Tony had had to face serious injury and he was understandably anxious about the surgery: "I was worried," Tony admitted. "I didn't like the thought of having any operation. I'd only been in hospital once before and that was to have my tonsils out when I was four, so I didn't look forward to it."

In the event the cartilage operation on 4th April (which kept Tony in hospital for a fortnight) forced Currie to sit out Sheffield United's tours of Algeria and Cyprus, Alf Ramsey's last match in charge of the national team and, to Tony's immense frustration, the entirety of Joe Mercer's seven-game reign as England's caretaker manager.

In stark contrast to both his predecessor and eventual successor (Don Revie), Joe Mercer, English football's favourite 'Uncle', had time for the free spirits of the English game as he proved with his selection of both Stan Bowles and Frank Worthington. Consequently, there is every reason to believe that Currie might have helped himself to another handful of caps during Mercer's stewardship; and who knows, possession of the shirt might have made it that much harder for Revie to disregard him as he subsequently did.

With his international future far from certain, Currie would receive more bad news at the start of the 1974-75 campaign, when both Dick Wragg and Maurice Board announced their intentions to stand down as Sheffield United's chairman and vice-chairman respectively.

Unfortunately, the new men in charge, John Hassall and Albert Jackson, did not honour Wragg's pledges to invest in the team.

In fairness to Hassall and Jackson, the reality of the situation, of course, was that with all available funds being set aside to pay for the construction of the new stand, United simply didn't have the money to make the necessary improvements to the playing side.

With the sale of Currie *verboten*, and having announced a trading loss of £170,000 at the end of the 1973-74 season, United simply couldn't afford to refuse the £160,000 that Stoke offered for Geoff Salmons in July 1974.

Salmons had been such an integral part of the Sheffield United team that supporters could only view his sale – which was, "purely for financial reasons" – with dismay. Currie was especially disappointed, complaining, with irrefutable logic, "How can you build when you sell your best players?"

Although Furphy was given some money to spend, splashing out £100,000 to lure forward Tony Field and diminutive left-sided midfield player David Bradford from his old club Blackburn Rovers and another midfielder, Tony Garbett, from Watford, several of the Bramall Lane old guard were not impressed that Furphy had gone shopping for new blood in the lower divisions, among them Tony Currie: "[Furphy] brought in players who'd been with him at Blackburn: Terry Garbett, Tony Field and David Bradford. I felt it was a bit like Cloughie doing what he did at Leeds and Furphy upset some of our players because there was a bit of a clique with him and those three players. Garbett and Bradford were great lads, but Tony Field was a bit difficult to take because he had an attitude. He was quite a skilful lad, but perhaps not a team player."

"They were good honest professionals," Len Badger summarises, "but they didn't have the quality."

Indeed, only one of Furphy's signings, Scottish goalkeeper Jim Brown (a £65,000 capture from Chesterfield) could be deemed to have been a success at the Lane.

"It was a difficult time at Bramall Lane," Currie explains, "because the building of the new South Stand, which took two years, meant there was little available cash to spend in the transfer market. Even so, we felt that we had a genuine chance of qualifying for Europe in the 1974-75 season, especially after making a good start to the season."

After only one defeat from their opening seven games (away at Derby County), a run which included four victories on the trot (against Newcastle United, Ipswich Town, West Ham and Middlesbrough), United then came crashing down to earth on 21st September when Leeds United trounced them 5-1 at Elland Road. "We were always liable to do that," Currie recalls philosophically, "because we were an attacking team, first and foremost. It was very difficult for us to play defensively with the players we had in the team, so it was always a good match to watch, whoever we played."

Despite the defeat at Leeds, a point away at Wolves and a home win against Liverpool (thanks to an Alan Woodward goal expertly set up by Currie with a remarkable defence-splitting long-range left-foot pass) United found themselves sitting in fifth place.

Although three defeats in four games (against Stoke, Derby and Leicester) saw the Blades drop down to ninth, wins against Birmingham, Carlisle and Luton and a 2-2 draw with Burnley propelled the Blades back into the top five.

Had they been able to push on from there, United might have been able to mount a serious challenge for the league title but once again the gloved hand of inconsistency came tapping on their shoulder with three defeats and only one win from their next six games, culminating in a bruising Boxing Day encounter with Middlesbrough at Ayresome Park.

"I counted eight cases of shirt pulling and nine deliberate trips on my players out there," Furphy complained after his team had been beaten 1-0. "Tony Currie was kicked five times and Len Badger has a broken nose."

Once again it had been a case of stop Currie and you stopped United, something to which Tony had become all too accustomed. "Teams would often stick somebody on me to try and cut out the supply to our forward line. It's very difficult to shrug somebody off when they're just following you and have no interest in the game. Their job is just to follow you about to try and make sure you don't get a kick. I wanted to be the best player every time, but there's always the other team trying to stop you, no matter how.

"At times, there were two men marking me and kicking me, and sometimes that tactic worked. If I did not perform, it wasn't a question of not wanting to know. People don't realise how bloody difficult it was sometimes."

In those days, of course, football was a genuine contact sport, a man's game, and Currie has always been keen to point out that he could dish out the physical stuff as well as take it. "I weren't a soft touch," he stresses. "You couldn't be in those days. I could handle myself. Don't you worry."

United stopped the rot with a 1-1 draw at home to Arsenal and a 2-0 win at home to Bristol City in the third round of the FA Cup in which Currie was at his imperious best, turning in a performance that was described by *The Green 'Un* as one of the finest individual displays Bramall Lane had ever seen.

"I had my doubts about Tony Currie before the match," Bristol City's skipper Geoff Merrick graciously applauded, "but one minute he can be walking along lazily with the ball, the next minute he's twisting his way through all [our] defenders to get a shot in. I am now a fan of his."

United stretched their unbeaten run with a 1-1 draw at home to Manchester City and an impressive 3-1 win away at Spurs but were then sent crashing down to earth on 25th January when, following an abject display, they were given a well-deserved 4-1 spanking away at Aston Villa in the fourth round of the FA Cup.

Following a disappointing home draw with league strugglers Luton Town on 1st February, Furphy evidently decided it was time to shake things up a little, stripping Currie of the captain's armband and handing it to Keith Eddy for the visit to Carlisle the following week.

To his great credit Currie refused to throw his crayons out of the pram and instead offered Eddy his full support. To be fair to Furphy, his plan worked as his team embarked on a run that would see them lose just two more games throughout the remainder of the season and saw Currie play some of the best football of his career to date, inspiring United to the very brink of European qualification.

His brilliance was never better captured than when the Blades entertained West Ham United on 22nd March – the game that marked Currie's 300th appearance in a Sheffield United shirt.

Suitably for such a landmark, Currie's performance that day was regarded as arguably his best ever for United and it was during this game that he scored the goal that will ensure his soccer immortality.

In what would prove to be a thrilling end-to-end contest, West Ham took an eighth-minute lead through Bobby Gould, a lead that lasted all of a minute when

United equalised following a move started and finished by Currie.

Currie whipped over an inch-perfect cross from the left flank, finding Alan Woodward on the opposite wing, whose shot was blocked. When Steve Cammack's follow-up hit the post and rolled across the line, Currie was on hand to nudge home the rebound. "It was my 50th league goal for United," Currie recalls, "so it was a bit special."

West Ham soon regained the lead, however, when United's keeper Jim Brown somehow contrived to spill Billy Jennings' innocuous-looking overhead kick into his own goal. As a result United went in at the break trailing 2-1.

Within 12 minutes of the restart, the Blades were back on terms through Alan Woodward – the 1000th, scored by United in the First Division in post-war years.

With United laying siege to the visitors' goal, first Currie and then Cammack hit the bar. Then, with only 11 minutes left on the clock, there seemed little indication of the individual brilliance that was to follow when Currie won a tackle inside the United half.

Tony himself picks up the story: "It started off with me winning the ball in a tackle about ten yards inside our own half. Everybody says I never used to tackle, but I've got video evidence to prove it! I block-tackled somebody right on the byline and the ball went to Cammack who played it to Woodward. Woody then played it back to me after I'd crept up to the halfway line. By the time I got up to the box, I was swaying this way and that before placing a left-foot shot into the corner of the net."

"A quality goal from a quality player," commentator John Motson memorably erupted – for Sheffield United fans a line as immortal as the one used by Kenneth

Wolstenholme to accompany Geoff Hurst's third and England's fourth goal in the 1966 World Cup Final.

Characteristically, Tony was humble about his wonder goal: "It wasn't a great strike on the ball but it still looked good on the telly.

"Although it was a bit of a zig-zag manoeuvre at the end of it, I didn't actually beat any players. Lots of people thought I'd beaten three or four players, but that wasn't the case. Kevin Lock just kept backing off and taking my dummies and kept going back onto the other foot. The goal has been shown many times on TV because the game was featured on *Match of the Day*. It was lucky because we rarely featured on *Match of the Day*. It was usually the big boys who were shown and we had to settle for appearing on Yorkshire TV on their Sunday programme."

In fact, Tony modestly believes that the goal's endurance has had more to do with Motson's spontaneous description of it than the goal itself and when Currie bumped into the commentator many years later in a pub in Herefordshire, Tony was delighted to offer his gratitude in person: "I was out with some friends when I saw him and we had a little chat about the game.

"I thanked him for coming up with a line that has helped us both... His comment has stuck ... and has helped develop an almost myth-like memory that it was a mazy dribble. In fact, although I ran a long way with the ball and played the odd one-two, the West Ham defenders kept backing off until I thought I might as well try my luck with my left foot. It wasn't the sweetest shot I ever hit but it left Mervyn Day flat-footed and found the bottom corner."

Despite chances at either end during the remaining minutes, Currie's "quality goal" proved to be the match winner, and to acknowledge what had been an inspired all-round display, the players walked off at the end of the match to 'You Can Do Magic' – Currie's signature tune.

"Currie was absolutely tremendous," West Ham boss John Lyall graciously acknowledged after the match. "I could not wish to see a better midfield display than that."

Speaking after the match, Keith Eddy also heaped praise on his team-mate, revealing that his and Currie's relationship had not suffered one bit since he had taken over the captaincy: "There have been no problems between me and TC. He has been marvellous and every time I have asked for something he has tried to give it. Saturday's match was [a great] example. On the day he was magnificent, the icing on the cake. I just kept telling the lads to give him the ball because I could see West Ham were frightened to death of him. Poor Tony was just worn out at the end of it all but what a performance!"

"TC is just magic," echoed *The Sheffield Star*. "If he goes on playing like this, England manager Don Revie just can't ignore him."

While Tony was delighted with his performance against the Hammers, later rating it as one of his three all-time finest, he realised that even if he played to that standard every time he stepped onto a football pitch it would make little or no difference to his international prospects: "It said in the match report in *The Sheffield Star* that it was a pity England manager Don Revie wasn't there to witness it. But it wouldn't have made any difference with Don."

In fact, displaying a perversity of selection that would be one of the hallmarks of his turbulent and unsuccessful reign, Revie had even recently announced that he would *not* be selecting the flair players he had at his disposal, the sort of players who would do the unexpected, and instead would be building his team around players who would give him one hundred per cent application and carry out his instructions.

After beating West Ham, Sheffield United found themselves a mere five points behind league leaders Everton with a game in hand. With eight games to go of a uniquely open and competitive season the league title remained within plausible reach. Sadly, a 2-2 draw at Coventry, a 1-0 defeat at Arsenal and a 1-1 at home to Leeds ensured it was not to be.

"We should have won the league," Ken Furphy believes to this day. "We lost it by drawing at Coventry and losing at Arsenal. They were fighting relegation and they were a disgrace. The first thing they did was kick Tony."

Despite the disappointment of missing out on the possibility of a title win, a European place remained a realistic and tantalisingly close prospect. Back to back wins at home against Stoke on 12th April and a remarkable 3-2 win a week later away at Everton after being two down at half-time (Currie setting up the two comeback goals and then scoring the winner with a superb left-footed half-volley), not only ended the title aspirations of the Potters and the Toffees respectively but pushed United within touching distance of their European dream.

Currie was at this stage playing the football of his life. One flash of genius during the Stoke game has lived long in the memory of Ken Furphy: "We were fourth, Stoke were fifth and Bramall Lane was full. We're 2-0 up and Tony gets the ball with his back to goal. Mike Pejic comes in from the rear and when Tony puts his foot on the ball [Pejic] dives in as if he wants to kill him. Everyone in the stand gasps because we can see Pejic coming but Tony knew he was there so he flicks the ball up and Pejic goes straight through and ends up flat on his back. Tony catches the ball as it comes down then stands on it again, blowing kisses at the crowd. Everyone is up on their feet but now there's another gasp because Denis Smith is flying in, mad as a hatter, so Tony just drags the ball back and Smith disappears past him on his backside. Wonderful!"

With Alan Hudson also in the Stoke line-up that day, it was clear from the first whistle that Currie was a man with a point to prove. The previous month Hudson had won his first cap for England and had impressed, earning raves for his performance in a rare 2-0 win over West Germany and it was clear he would retain his place when England entertained Cyprus four days after this game at Bramall Lane.

In the event Currie completely overshadowed his rival, seemingly spending the majority of the game looking for Hudson just so he could nutmeg him and blow kisses to the crowd.

A fortnight later, in United's penultimate game of the season against Leicester City, Currie left Bramall Lane with memories of an entirely different stripe when he was involved in what must surely be the most bizarre and misunderstood episode of his eventful career.

Leicester had arrived at Bramall Lane as cannon fodder. Having effectively avoided relegation the Foxes had little to play for (they finished the season in 18th place) while United still had a good chance of qualifying for Europe.

Indeed, the Blades had surged into a 4-0 lead (with Currie netting United's third with a precise 25-yard left-footed strike) when "the incident" that has so steadfastly refused to go away occurred.

When Leicester's Alan Birchenall surged through the middle of the park and into United's penalty area Currie tracked back to put in a tackle during which the pair collided with each other.

Currie and Birchenall collapsed side by side on the bone-hard pitch, and, before helping each other up, shared a moment of spontaneous on-field levity typical of two inveterate showmen.

"I was back in my own area doing a bit of defending," Currie reminisces, "which, in those days, fans will tell you probably wasn't like me at all! Me and Birch just collided as we went for the ball and we ended up sat on our backsides next to each other, having done a head-over-heels somersault. We just looked at one another and laughed. Then Birch said to me 'Give us a kiss, TC.' So I did. We had been mates for a good few years before that. But you could say we were never closer than in that split second... After the kiss, we just got up and carried on with the game."

Unbeknownst to the pair, a *Sunday Mirror* snapper had captured the smacker, and Birchenall and Currie were front-page news, much to the dismay of Birchenall's wife. "I woke up the next morning expecting my normal Sunday cuppa," Birchenall chuckled, "but when the bedroom door opened my wife threw the paper at me instead. It looked as if we were giving each other deep throat!

"As I recall, all hell broke loose after the picture hit the papers," Birchenall continues. "It was on the main news bulletins and a question was asked in the House of Commons about what sport was coming to. I got besieged, TC got besieged. I had letters from right-wing groups saying that, when they came to power, perverts like me and Tony would be put up against a wall and shot!"

When the photograph was duly disseminated around the globe, Currie and Birchenall became, for a short while, improbable gay icons, particularly in Germany when one of Deutschland's top-shelf publications, *International Man*, reprinted it.

"I received all sorts of mail," Birchenall revealed to *The Sun* in 2005. "A German gay news magazine even wrote to me, asking if I'd do a column for them. The picture won a major award and they wanted me and TC to go to Paris to collect it. But we declined. People were on to us straight after. In the end, we must have spent a fortnight trying to tell everyone that we were not of that persuasion! In that split second of actually doing it, though, I never even thought about the gay thing."

"Birch is right when he talks of the uproar it caused," Currie added in 2005. "Even now I still find myself having to explain to people who ask about that kiss that we are not a couple and never have been. In fact, whenever me and Birch go out together socially these days we always make sure our wives come with us – just to be on the safe side."

"Me and Tony did it instinctively," Birchenall explains. "But looking at the photograph, there were two guys both with long blond hair kissing each other on the lips. We were athletes, footballers and there had never been a picture like it. But 30 years ago? Bloody hell, that is hard to believe, as there is never a day goes by without someone having a bit of banter with me about it. We've a big picture of it in our club lounge at the Walkers Stadium and the lads have told me it was voted one of the top five kisses on Sky recently. Today, everyone kisses. But back then it was a no-no. Yet me and TC weren't at all embarrassed, because that is our sense of humour. Tony went on to become a great player, while the things I'm known for are kissing Tony Currie and scoring a goal against Leeds. That's my claim to fame! It's amazing, though, how many people who were not even born then have seen that picture – and how many still have prints of it 30 years on and send it to me to sign. Sometimes I go to do an after-dinner job and they don't know what to say to introduce me. They can hardly go on about my England Under-23 caps, so they introduce me as 'Alan Birchenall, remembered for a goal against Leeds and kissing Tony Currie.' It encapsulates my 18-year playing career. That picture sums up my outlook on life. I like a laugh.

"Over the years, people have started to see it for what it was – an instinctive thing between two buddies. I'm pleased I did it and, if I am to be remembered for anything, I'd like to be remembered as a footballer who enjoyed having fun playing the game I loved."

Currie remains equally happy to have played his part in creating an enduring piece of footballing folklore: "Me and Birch were acknowledged as two of the more flamboyant and extrovert players of the 1970s. Yet despite what it looks like on that photograph, we certainly weren't a pair of dumb blondes. We always have a laugh about it and I can guarantee there's not a week goes by even now without somebody coming up to me and asking, 'Who was the geezer you kissed at Bramall Lane all those years ago?' I never dreamed at the time it would have the kind of lasting impact it has."

When all the brouhaha had died down, Currie and Sheffield United still had the serious business of a place in Europe to challenge for.

With their nearest rivals all having finished their campaigns, everything hinged on United's last game of the season: an away fixture at Birmingham City. The Blades arrived at St Andrew's knowing that a win would clinch for the club an historic UEFA Cup place.

Unfortunately, it wasn't to be United's night as a 0-0 draw left them just one point, or one goal, short of their dream. Instead United and Currie in particular were left to rue missed chances, as full-back Len Badger explains: "We needed two points at Birmingham and we ended up drawing after Tony Currie missed a sitter. He went round three people and side-footed the ball past the post. It was late on in the game and if that had gone in, we'd have been playing in Europe. I'll never forgive TC for denying me the chance to play in Europe!"

Nevertheless, United's sixth place finish, a mere four points behind champions Derby County, represented United's highest league finish for 13 years, and an achievement that Sheffield United have not equalled or bettered since.

"We certainly caused a few raised eyebrows by finishing sixth," Tony remarked at the end of the campaign, "and the way were playing it was a shame the season ended when it did. We lost only two of our last 15 matches and were going so strongly it would have been interesting to see where we would have finished if the campaign had lasted just another month."

Had United beaten Derby in their home fixture and merely drawn with the Rams at the Baseball Ground, United would have won the league by a point, an itch which Currie seems unable to scratch to this very day.

"People forget that, at one stage, we came within four points of being crowned champions," he reflected in 2014. "It was a tight race that year and I still maintain that, if we'd have had a few more players to cope with injuries, we'd have done it and what an achievement that would have been. Unfortunately, we lost to Derby home and away and that was the difference between first and sixth. We had folk like Woody, Eddie Colquhoun, Ted Hemsley and Badge in the side and, between all of us, we felt as if we could beat anyone at any given time. It didn't matter who they were, we knew we had it within us to come out on top."

Such was the buzz around Sheffield United that a few pundits (notably Jimmy Hill) even tipped United as an outside bet for the championship title the following season.

At Bramall Lane, however, there was a nagging suspicion of shortcomings within the team that badly needed attention. One of those who shared these doubts was long-serving full-back Len Badger: "We finished sixth, but we won so many games we didn't deserve to win. It was one of those freaks. The writing was on the wall because we were getting away with bloody murder."

Furthermore with so many key players the wrong side of 30 years of age, it was evident that the need to substantially strengthen the team had now become a matter of no small urgency.

Sadly with the new stand to finance, the budget for new players, or at least ones good enough to help maintain United's First Division status, was virtually non-existent. Although United did at last have a good crop of youngsters in reserve, the most promising of them – Keith Edwards, Simon Stainrod and Tony Kenworthy – were not introduced until the end of the season.

With the club desperately short of funds, chairman John Hassall asked Furphy if he would be prepared to take the team on a money-spinning pre-season tour of Tunisia. Fearing a disruption to his pre-season training schedule and aware that any injuries would stretch his thin squad to breaking point, Furphy declined.

"It was worth about £10,000 to the club," Furphy later explained, "but I said, 'No way,' we needed a month's training to gradually get harder or we'd be getting injuries. A board meeting decided in his favour and, in Tunisia, three players got injured. In the first few games of the new season we had three reserves in."

Furphy's fragile relationship with his chairman was stretched further during the club's protracted negotiations to buy Southend United's target man Chris Guthrie as a replacement for injured striker Billy Dearden.

"Guthrie had scored a lot of goals for Southend," laments Furphy. "I bid £40,000; they said, forget it. So I did. Then United's chairman, John Hassall, phones me, asking me, did I get permission from the board to approach a player? The Southend chairman had been onto him. He wants to interfere, but I'm having to explain the nature of the game and how you always offer less than you're prepared to pay. He then tells me to come with him to meet the Southend chairman on the motorway. Anyway, in some motel I said '£50,000 plus Terry Nicholl.' Southend said, 'No way': they wanted £90,000. I said to the chairman, 'Let's go; he's not worth it.' He then says, 'Okay, we'll give you £90,000.' I looked at him and said, 'Are you sure?' He says to me, 'You want him, don't you?' I said, 'I do, but not at that price.' The chairman bought him in effect, not me."

Suspension kept Currie out of the opening day of the 1975-76 season, ruling him out of the game that saw Bramall Lane finally inaugurate the new South Stand – an auspicious 1-1 draw against Derby County, the reigning First Division champions, and a game that United were actually unfortunate not to have won.

Few of the 31,000 gate, however, could have predicted what lay in store for United over the coming months, although when United's defensive linchpin John Flynn dislocated his shoulder in the second game (a 3-1 defeat at home to Arsenal), putting him out of action for several weeks, the portents were not good.

Despite these two early setbacks, Tony remained optimistic about the forthcoming season: "I still think we will give the fans plenty to cheer about. No other team will have an easy time against us – believe me… After all, we have some terrific players – like goalkeeper Jim Brown,

Tony Field, and the ever-dangerous Alan Woodward – and we really believe in ourselves… All things considered, I'm sure we are going to have another great season and perhaps even win something. That is what we really want. United are overdue for a success."

Currie returned to the side for the third game of the season: a tricky away tie against newly promoted Manchester United, the club for whom he had almost signed the previous season.

In front of a vociferous 56,000 crowd celebrating Manchester United's first home game back in the top flight, the Old Trafford outfit romped to a comprehensive 5-1 victory.

Two more defeats at the hands of Everton and Leeds followed to leave Sheffield United marooned at the foot of the league table – the position they would occupy without interruption for the rest of the season.

Bizarrely, despite his reputation for picking form players, England manager Don Revie chose this moment to hand Tony an international recall, awarding him his seventh cap in the match against Switzerland on 3rd September, which England won 2-1 with goals from Keegan and Channon.

* * * * *

When Currie returned from England duty, Sheffield United were still rooted to the bottom of the table and were looking more like relegation fodder with every game. Although the early season injury crisis abated, after eight games Sheffield United had scored only three goals – two of them Keith Eddy spot kicks!

Although there were many who believed Furphy was eminently capable of turning United's fortunes around, the manager's cause was hardly helped by rapidly deteriorating relationships with both the chairman John Hassall *and* his star player.

Furphy had been particularly distressed by Tony's eating habits. "He used to get on the coach with a pocket full of chocolate caramels," Furphy elucidates, "and wolf them down like a compulsive eater, so we were forever trying to keep his weight down. It was all part of that nervous disposition. He also developed this habit during games of going down and not getting back up. One day it cost us a goal against West Ham so I turned to the chairman and told him if he did it again I'd have to pull him off."

".... [John] Hassall told me not to because it would devalue his transfer price," Furphy later recalled. "This was news to me! Anyway, I pulled him off." It was the first time in Currie's Sheffield United career that he'd been substituted.

Rather than throwing his shirt to the floor, telephoning a taxi and airing his grievances in the tabloids, Tony was honest enough to tacitly admit that the manager had been right, rationalising his mid-game inertia thus: "I want to be perfection," he told *The Observer*. "I'm disgusted with myself if I give a bad ball. I feel I've failed. I just stand still and let the play go on past me."

Although Currie has never devalued the positive influence Furphy had on his career, the pair did not always enjoy the smoothest of relationships.

One minute Furphy would be handing Currie the Sheffield United club captaincy and giving him pep-talks about his future, buttering his ego with talk about him one day skippering England and being an international for years to come; the next minute he was singling Tony out for unfair criticism, on one occasion claiming that his star player lacked motivation and was a poor trainer – accusations that Currie has always vehemently disputed.

On yet another Furphy tattled to United's directors that Currie had failed to follow instructions during a match. Again, Currie has always defended himself against such calumnies; after all it was not always easy to play each game according to the drawing board when faced each week with the rabid attentions of some of the most effective hatchet men the English game has ever produced.

For a man who had handed Currie the captain's armband with the expressed intention of boosting his international prospects, such accusations were extremely counter-productive. Certainly making it public that he had failed to carry out instructions was hardly going to *enhance* his standing with Don Revie, for whom such discipline was of paramount importance.

"When I was reunited with Furphy five years after leaving Watford," Currie remarks, "I didn't feel that I had anything to prove to him because by now I was an England international at the top of my game. He did try to put me down a few times; why, I don't know, perhaps because I was idolised and he wanted to be."

Currie's substitution against West Ham only served to heighten the rumours (that had latterly re-appeared in the press) that he was on his way out of Bramall Lane.

Although it was said that Furphy's sacking a fortnight later was precipitated rather more by the fact that United were glued to the bottom of the league and his signing of York City's Cliff Calvert (a move which chairman Hassall had allegedly opposed and had not, in fact, officially sanctioned), the decision to undermine the team's talisman against West Ham had certainly been a contributory factor. As a parade of Newcastle United managers who dared to drop Alan Shearer would discover over 25 years later – the price you pay for wounding the supporters' darling is invariably your job.

Bizarrely, one of Furphy's last acts as Sheffield United manager was to re-appoint Currie as team captain in the absence of Keith Eddy for the trip to Birmingham City. Sadly the placatory offer of the armband was unable to galvanise Currie into match-winning form and United's ninth defeat of the season was Furphy's last game as Sheffield United manager. To the dismay of incredulous fans, two days later, on 6th October, the man who had guided Sheffield United to within a point of European competition earlier in the year was summarily dismissed.

The Bramall Lane hot seat would prove to be Furphy's last managerial job in English football. Instead Furphy headed for the North American Soccer League to manage the New York Cosmos whose side included the legendary Pele, a player to whom Furphy believed Currie compared favourably: "Pele played for me at New York Cosmos and Tony was very similar, better in some ways. Pele couldn't keep the ball as long with people snapping at his heels!"

After a nine-day interregnum during which John Harris and coach Cec Coldwell ran team affairs, on 16th October 1975, 53-year-old Notts County supremo Jimmy Sirrel was appointed as Furphy's successor.

While Sirrel had performed minor miracles on a shoestring budget at Notts County, guiding them from the lower reaches of the Fourth Division to the brink of the First Division, the Scot's reputation, sadly, would not be enhanced during his brief time at Bramall Lane.

Sirrel's first order of business was to dispel any notions that Currie was for sale, despite the fact that Tony had submitted a written transfer request to the Sheffield United chairman amid widely publicised interest from Leeds United, who, it was rumoured, were so keen to land

Currie that they were prepared to offer Duncan McKenzie and Billy Bremner in part exchange, though both clubs officially denied this.

"Tony Currie wants to leave Bramall Lane but the board have turned him down," *The Sheffield Star* reported on 17th October. "And Jimmy Sirrel, appointed as manager of Sheffield United yesterday was the first to be told of the situation, although he took no part in the decision. Chairman John Hassall, who told Currie of the board's verdict, stated: 'Currie's written request was turned down by the directors at their meeting yesterday. I have seen Currie and told him that I expect him and all other members of the staff to co-operate with our new manager Mr Sirrel to pull Sheffield United out of our present difficulties.'"

Second order of business for Sirrel was to initiate a clear out of the playing staff. Before 1975 was out popular servants Len Badger (who was transferred to Chesterfield in January 1976), Ted Hemsley (who lost his place in the side) and Billy Dearden (who was sent out on loan and then transferred permanently to Chester in February 1976) had all played their last games for United, with Keith Eddy also bidding farewell a few weeks into the New Year, joining Furphy at New York Cosmos.

With no sizeable pot of gold placed at his disposal to strengthen the demoralised squad he'd inherited from Furphy, Sirrel was restricted to only two signings: left-back Paul Garner, a shrewd £59,555 capture from Huddersfield (to replace Hemsley); and, on a free transfer from Celtic, the legendary Scottish winger and alumnus of the Lisbon Lions, Jimmy Johnstone.

With the departures of Badger, Hemsley, Eddy and Dearden, a large portion of the dressing room spirit went with them and in their place came a group of players who didn't seem to share the same visceral feeling for the club, at least as far as newcomer Jimmy Johnstone was concerned.

"A lot of them were mercenaries," claimed Johnstone (who himself later admitted to treating his time at Bramall Lane as one long drinking binge). "Don't get me wrong, they were all good lads and I got on well with them, but they all seemed just to be after making a few quid then gettin' away. I wasn't used to this. I'd played at Celtic with passion; at Sheffield it was a merry-go-round. They'd sit in the dressing room talking about who was after them: there was no loyalty. I'd no idea of a football club like this."

Although Johnstone didn't name names, Currie was one of the keenest to get away. Indeed, Jimmy Sirrel had barely been in the job a month when he had to turn down a *second* transfer request from his star player, who this time risked both disciplinary action and the wrath of United fans by making his restlessness public.

If Currie thought his miserable season couldn't get any worse, he was wrong. In November, Currie dutifully reported for England duty for the crunch, win-or-bust European Championship qualifier against Portugal. After watching the wretched 1-1 draw (which effectively ended England's interest in the competition) from the substitutes' bench, Tony began complaining of internal pains.

When his condition worsened during the flight back from Lisbon, Currie was taken in a wheelchair, as soon as the plane touched down in Heathrow, to a chauffeur-driven car via which he was rushed back to Sheffield accompanied by Sir Andrew Stephen, the president of the Football Association, and Len Shipman, the president of the Football League. After being diagnosed with acute appendicitis by Sheffield United's club doctor, Professor

Frank O'Gorman, Tony was rushed to the Sheffield Royal Infirmary, dramatically arriving there mere minutes before his appendix burst. Although the subsequent emergency operation was completed without complications, Currie was initially ruled out of action for several weeks.

In the event a miraculous recovery ensured he would miss only four league games, the first of which – a 2-1 defeat at Stoke City – saw Jimmy Johnstone make his United debut. If Sirrel was pinning his hopes on the mercurial former Scottish international it was a gamble that spectacularly backfired. Indeed, by the time Currie returned to the first team on 20th December, Johnstone had already been dropped and would only feature twice more throughout the remainder of the campaign, and in only a handful of games the following season.

It had soon become apparent that Sirrel's appointment had been a mistake for everyone concerned. Sirrel, it is said, almost immediately regretted leaving his beloved Notts County.

"He would say to us in team talks," Jimmy Johnstone recalled, "'I can always return to the house on the hill.' I think that was Notts County! No one knew for sure! You'd look round and see players looking the other way."

Furthermore, Sirrel quickly realised that the task of saving United from relegation with the players and financial resources available was an impossible task, a task made all the more difficult by his failure to win over the hearts and minds of his new charges.

The departing Len Badger offers this opinion: "Jimmy Sirrel was a good, honest man, but there was something missing. He wanted big, strong types who could whack it up and get up and down the pitch." Certainly this was not the sort of football on which Bramall Lane regulars had been weaned under John Harris.

While Currie claims to have liked Sirrel personally, he concedes that he often found his training methods wearying and uninspired: "I got on well with Jimmy. He'd had Don Masson at Notts County and he compared me to him. The only thing with Jimmy was that he loved practice matches, so we seemed to play them from Monday to Friday and then had to go out on Saturday and do the same thing."

After 22 games, Sheffield United had succumbed to an embarrassing 18 defeats, accumulating a desultory five points – a new league record. The optimism of the pre-season had given way to fatalism.

"We just got into a rut and couldn't get out of it," Currie explains. "We were getting regular thrashings, it seemed almost weekly, and it was a very depressing time. My game was suffering as well."

With his close friends Hemsley, Dearden and Badger no longer around, coupled with the unsettling effects of Leeds United's pursuit of his signature, it was perhaps inevitable that Currie's loyalties and motivation would soften and on 31st January, following his side's defeat away at Arsenal (the 22nd game in a run of 23 games without a win for the Blades) he handed in another transfer request, reportedly his third in four months. Little remembered now is the fact that Alan Woodward, the club's longest-serving player following Badger's departure, chose the same day to do likewise.

Although United finally returned to winning ways with a 2-1 victory at home to Aston Villa on Valentine's Day 1976, two draws and four more defeats from their next six league games finally put the Blades out of their misery.

By the time relegation was mathematically confirmed at the end of March they had won only two games and

Currie, aged 17, in his Watford days (Colorsport)

Sheffield United photocall, 1970 (Colorsport)

Tony Currie and Alan Woodward look on as George Best shows Len Badger a clean pair of heels at Old Trafford, 2nd October 1971 (Colorsport)

Currie giving Bryan 'Pop' Robson the runaround – Sheffield United v West Ham United, 29th February 1972 (Colorsport)

Currie strikes an iconic pose for Sheffield United, 2nd August 1972 (Colorsport)

Tony Currie plays with the late Trevor Hockey's beard whilst the late Alan Woodward looks on – Sheffield United photocall, 3rd August 1972 (Colorsport)

Currie does his best to evade the close attention of two Spurs defenders, 23rd December 1972 (Colorsport)

Currie in action for England whilst winning his third cap against Italy, 14th June 1973 (Colorsport)

Currie skippers the Blades at Old Trafford ahead of Bobby Charlton's last home game for Manchester United – 23rd April 1973 (Colorsport)

Disaster for England – despite Currie's best efforts England fail to qualify for the 1974 World Cup (Colorsport)

Tony doubles up with his pal the late Alan Ball during an England training session, January 1974 (Colorsport)

In action for Leeds United against Chelsea, 2nd September 1978 (Colorsport)

Currie adroitly evades a flying Tommy Smith challenge – Leeds United v Liverpool (Colorsport)

In action for Leeds United v Everton, 21st April 1979 (Colorsport)

Getting stuck in for Queens Park Rangers v Notts County, 14th February 1981 (Colorsport)

In full flow for England against Wales, 23rd May 1979 (Colorsport)

Heading for a 50-50 with Tottenham's Tony Galvin in the 1982 FA Cup Final (Colorsport)

Currie leads his team-mates out at Wembley in the 1982 FA Cup Final replay (Colorsport)

*Signing for Torquay United in 1984
(Torbay News Agency)*

*Tony and Alan Birchenall recreate "that
kiss" in front of a blow-up of the original
smooch in 2012 (Leicester Mercury)*

Tony in the suite named in his honour at Bramall Lane (Martyn Harrison)

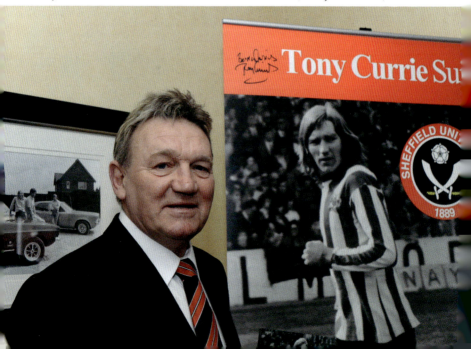

only four subsequent victories after their fate had been sealed spared them the ignominy of recording the lowest ever points total in the top flight!

Having scored just 33 league goals during the entire season it didn't take a genius to work out what had been at the heart of United's problems. The club's new striker, Chris Guthrie had proved to be a costly flop; nine goals from 37 league matches being a measly return for his £90,000 transfer fee.

"Chris Guthrie was brought in over the summer for around £100,000 and that proved to be a waste of money," Currie later sighed. "He was very good in the air, but that was about it because he wasn't mobile. He certainly wasn't a Billy Dearden."

That said, it had also been a lean season for Currie in front of goal. Despite missing only nine matches throughout the season, he scored only one goal – at Norwich in April – and he admitted even that was a bit of a fluke!

* * * * *

In the immediate aftermath of what he would describe as the hardest and most frustrating season of his career, Currie's future remained unresolved. The big question was: would he stay or would he go?

In the event Currie remained a Blade until June, travelling to Gibraltar with the rest of the United squad for a post-season mini-tournament involving Lincoln City and Wolverhampton Wanderers. After beating Lincoln 6-5 on penalties in the semi-final, United met Wolves in the final only to be spanked 4-1.

The match against Wolves proved to be Currie's last appearance as a Sheffield United player and when he returned from Gibraltar, months of distracting conjecture, rumour and speculation were brought to an end.

"I was on an end-of-season trip in Gibraltar with the team," Currie recalls, "and I was told [by Jimmy Sirrel] to go and report to John Harris when I got back. Nobody told me why and I didn't ask, because you didn't in those days. You just got on with it. So I went to John Harris's house when I got back and I still didn't ask any questions. Forty-five minutes later we were driving into Leeds United. I still didn't ask John what was going on. I didn't want to. Maybe I was scared.

"Even when we drove through those [Elland Road] gates I didn't think the club would let me go. It hadn't sunk in what was happening. Then John Harris let me go in and see Jimmy Armfield and, by the time I'd come out, I'd signed. I think John was a bit taken aback because I'd done it and they'd lost me."

While there is no doubt that Sheffield United would have preferred to have kept Currie to help them win promotion back to the First Division, the board were sensitive to the need to cash in on their most valuable asset in order to give Sirrel the financial resources to rebuild for the following season. Leeds were offering ten times the fee the Blades had paid to Watford in 1968. It was an offer the Sheffield club simply couldn't refuse.

It's a salient point that Tony has always been keen to stress: "My answer to people who say I left a sinking ship at Sheffield United," he argued in October 1976, "I say only one thing to that – it had already sunk when I went."

"A lot of people thought I deserted United, but I'd signed a six-year contract two years before I left and not many people sign a contract of that length. I'd have probably ended up signing another one after that, but we got relegated and I couldn't afford to stay any longer because I was an England international and I didn't want to lose that. I thought it was time to go after nine years at the club. You can't take a chance and think you're going to come straight back up again.

"I didn't really want to leave because I'm not the type who likes to move around. I don't like different environments. But at the same time I wanted to be with a club that was capable of winning trophies.

"I felt [Leeds] were going places," Tony stated, "and I was so confident of their ability that I tossed away a guaranteed £20,000 testimonial and moved to Leeds for the same wage. The money didn't come into the move – I just wanted to try and win something. It's a shame that didn't happen at Bramall Lane – but I don't think anyone can accuse me of being overambitious."

When Currie's move was finalised on 8th June, it was left to Jimmy Sirrel to placate United's heartbroken fans: "This has been a rather traumatic season for Sheffield United. One thing has led to another, culminating in relegation. There is no doubt that we have lost a tremendous asset, our club captain and an England international. In my job one has to take decisions and sometimes they are decisions that one would rather not have to make at all, but we have done what we believe to be right in view of all the circumstances of our club at this time. Negotiations went through very smoothly and amicably, probably helped because Manny Cussins is a former Sheffield man."

After one final journey to Bramall Lane to collect his boots and say goodbye to old friends, Currie was gone. As an illustration of his iconic status at Bramall Lane, within weeks of his departure, t-shirts went on sale bearing Tony's likeness and the legend, "Gone but not forgotten."

For Sheffield United it was the end of an era, and although the likes of Flynn, Colquhoun and Woodward remained for a few more seasons, the start of the 1979-80 season found the Blades in the Third Division (the club's first ever season outside the top two divisions). At the end of the 1980-81 season – ten years after Currie had helped the club secure promotion to the top flight on a wave of genuine optimism – relegation to the Fourth Division saw the club hit rock bottom.

Currie had made 313 league appearances for the Blades, scored 54 goals, assisted in dozens more, helped United become one of the best six teams in the country (in 1975) and left a treasure trove of indelible memories – and it's a genuine cultural tragedy that so few of them are preserved on video.

While his time at Leeds ultimately brought him a few shades closer to winning the domestic honours he craved and saw him earn more England caps than he did during his years at Bramall Lane, it is as a Sheffield United player that Currie will arguably be best remembered by the man on the Clapham Omnibus, a fact Currie has always acknowledged.

"I think my heart's really at Sheffield United," Currie stated in 1995. "I had nine years there and I had a great relationship with the crowd, although I did at all my clubs. But Sheffield United was my club."

"I spent my formative years and a long time here," Tony added in 2006. "You can't do that without it leaving a mark and that's why United will always be my club. I've got a real emotional attachment to this place and that's never going to change now. Obviously you always have affection for [all] your old clubs and I'm no different. But it's not the same as what I feel for United."

While it's now almost 40 years since Currie last played for Sheffield United, Blades supporters have never forgotten his contributions. In fact, when BBC South

Yorkshire carried out a poll of Blades fans in April 2004 to find out who they regarded as their team's greatest ever player, Currie won by a country mile – receiving almost twice as many votes as Brian Deane in second place (legendary inside-forward Jimmy Hagan was voted third greatest, with Alan Woodward coming in fourth). The following March, when BBC's *Football Focus* asked fans of every English and Scottish league club to nominate their all-time Cult Hero, Currie again came top of the Sheffield United poll with 53% of the vote.

Currie has always been both honoured and humbled by the comparison with Hagan: "To be mentioned in the same breath as Jimmy Hagan when people talk about United's greatest-ever players is some tribute. Not that I ever saw Jimmy play, but it's what you hear from people about how great he was."

To this very day Sheffield United fans of the early 1970s vintage only to have to hear 'You Can do Magic' and the memories of Currie at his impudent best come racing back, likewise for Tony himself.

"When I hear the song, it always brings back great memories," Currie reminisces. "You can never replace the buzz you got from playing football. Just to be out there, showing 20,000–30,000 people what you can do... I used to blow kisses to the crowd. I could hear everything the fans were saying to me and I always had a bit of banter with them. I think that's what they enjoyed. It was a fantastic time because we were a great team of friends and all got on fantastically well."

"We all loved each other and you don't get much of that nowadays."

7

1976–78

*"Finding new blood had to be a priority
and my first major signing, in June 1976,
needed to be a good one. It was."*

— Jimmy Armfield

CURRIE might have left Sheffield United to win trophies, but although Leeds were demonstrably a bigger club than their rivals down the M1 in those days, in actual fact, Tony arrived at Elland Road to find his new club in the middle of a period of, that dreaded word, transition.

The Don Revie era had come to an end when the former Leeds boss had accepted the England job and the man charged with recapturing the glory years was former England captain and ex-Bolton manager Jimmy Armfield (succeeding Brian Clough whose spell in charge at Elland Road had lasted a torrid 44 days). In his first season in charge, Armfield had guided Leeds to the European Cup Final, where, against Bayern Munich, his team had been desperately unfortunate to lose to goals from Franz Roth and Gerd Muller and some controversial and downright suspect decisions from French referee Michel Kitabdjian.

Currie liked the cut of the avuncular Armfield's jib. Upon meeting him for the first time, Tony told the press that his new boss was, "A very nice, quiet man."

While Armfield had inherited a star-studded team of internationals – and, in Billy Bremner and Johnny Giles, arguably the most effective and redoubtable central midfield pairing in Europe – he had also inherited an ageing team, the dismantling of which would cast a shadow over his time in charge at Elland Road. It was an unpleasant, but necessary task that Don Revie, incidentally, always maintained *he* would have found near impossible!

"Reshaping the Leeds playing staff was an incredibly tough proposition," Armfield explains in his autobiography. "Some of the players had been among the best in Europe and were virtually irreplaceable. How could any manager find another pairing like Bremner and Giles? They were unique and finding players remotely good enough to take their places was difficult at any price. But the job had to be done, step by cautious step, retaining some semblance of continuity while introducing players who would be the club's future."

The exodus began in March 1975 when England left-back Terry Cooper joined Jack Charlton at Middlesbrough, followed by the great Johnny Giles who left to become player-manager at West Bromwich Albion in July 1975; while the influential Mick Jones had retired in October 1975.

The following summer, fans' favourite Duncan McKenzie (a Clough signing) also departed, joining Anderlecht for £200,000, as did Terry Yorath who joined Coventry City for £125,000.

Currie barely had time to memorise the combination on his locker before two more Revie legends had emptied theirs. Bremner ended his 17-year association with the club when he signed for Hull City in September and then Norman Hunter also moved on, joining Bristol City for £40,000 in October.

Fortunately the return from injury of Eddie Gray and the retention of talented stalwarts such as David Harvey, Peter Lorimer, Allan Clarke, Trevor Cherry, Paul Madeley and Paul Reaney ensured a semblance of continuity.

While Armfield had enjoyed success as a player with Blackpool and as manager of Bolton Wanderers in the lower leagues, the sheer size of Leeds United often took him by surprise, as underlined to him by the process of signing Tony Currie.

"I had enjoyed success at Blackpool and Bolton but I had not experienced anything the size of Leeds. One example of the difference occurred in June 1976 when we went in for Tony Currie of Sheffield United, who was available at £250,000. I offered £220,000 and Maurice Lindley said, 'What are you playing at? If they want £250,000 give 'em £250,000. Don't mess about for the sake of 30 grand. Get it spent! He'll bring in that much through the gate at his first game.' To Blackpool and Bolton, £30,000 was a hell of a lot of money."

Although the fee that took Currie to Elland Road was actually reported as being *£240,000* the fee was still a big one, exceeding the £225,000 that Brian Clough had paid for Duncan McKenzie, making Currie Leeds' then most expensive signing, a fact not lost on the player himself.

"That's a lot of money," Tony gulped when he saw the amount of noughts on the cheque. "You'll be worth it," Armfield assured him. "After selling McKenzie we needed someone with charisma," Armfield explained. "Currie provided loads of it but I would not have signed him on charisma alone – I was convinced he was the genuine article as a player."

"Tony is the type of player we have needed since Johnny Giles left," Armfield told the press. "He is potentially the greatest midfield player in Great Britain. A classy performer who will give us that extra spark and midfield strength. I believe we can help Tony as much as he will help us."

Armfield's assistant, Don Howe, was also a confirmed fan. "The word 'great' must not be overused," Howe told reporters at Leeds' training ground. "We are too ready to describe good players as great ones and there are only a very few of them; but I know Tony Currie has the ability to become real quality."

Although Currie had been bought to add a dash of glamour, flair and subtlety, Howe was also quick to scotch the notion that they'd bought a fancy Dan. "There is nothing wrong with Tony's application or work-rate, either in training or matches. He works tremendously hard.

"When I think of the great midfielders, I always think of Johnny Giles first. He was the best I've ever seen, a man with all the attributes that a midfielder needs, and Tony will rank alongside him one day."

To help Tony's assimilation into his new team of super-fit, non-stop *übermenschen*, Armfield's first piece of advice to Currie when he arrived at Elland Road was to "cut out some of the showmanship". It was a recommendation that Tony was glad to accept.

"I could understand how [Jimmy Armfield] felt," Currie told the *Football Handbook* periodical in 1978. "He had paid Sheffield United his highest ever fee for me – and he wanted to show the fans that he'd bought an action man, not a playboy. So I got stuck in, trained hard and tried to fit into the Elland Road pattern."

In actual fact, Currie found it easy to settle in at Leeds, and having played with the likes of Clarke, Hunter and Madeley for England certainly helped.

"I fitted in straight away at Leeds, taking the place of Johnny Giles," Tony remarked. "I was a very similar player to him, spraying the ball about. There were a number of international players in the side who were still great players despite the fact they were getting on.

"I didn't feel any pressure replacing Johnny Giles," Currie added, "because I knew I had ability. I wasn't like Duncan McKenzie. He used to strut about, but Duncan wasn't a team man and I was. It was a myth that I was lazy.

"You have to remember that Leeds had always liked a bit of showmanship. Billy and John were like that. Take that game when they murdered Southampton and they were taking the Mick with their flicks and back heels. That was brilliant, but even so, they'd still never had anyone like me before."

Ironically, Currie's first game for Leeds was against Giles' West Bromwich Albion. The press inevitably billed it as a showdown between the two schemers – the former Leeds number ten and the present incumbent, the old master and the pretender to the throne.

Far from being overawed by the face-off, Currie couldn't wait to test himself against his predecessor. "I shall not be tempted to go out and prove who is best," Currie excitedly told *The Yorkshire Post*. "Giles used to move around all over the field and that is what I'll be doing. I don't mind playing on the left as I have a free role like Giles to spray the ball around. Giles was so consistent at passing the ball at any distance, but I can do that. I can hit anything I want."

Currie also boldly predicted he'd make a goalscoring start to his Leeds career: "I'll be sick if I don't get a goal. I've scored on all my debuts apart from the one for England – and that doesn't count because they took me off too early!"

Although Currie did not score, he did more than enough to impress in an entertaining 2-2 draw.

"Leeds looked less like a team than at any other time Giles has graced Elland Road," *The Yorkshire Post*'s Barry Foster opined, "with only Tony Currie displaying the class of the old Leeds. He must have wondered where all the stars had gone. He did everything right, but had so little help from his team-mates. He gave total commitment for 90 minutes, his shooting being a particularly forceful part of his game, but even in the days of John Charles, Leeds found one man could not do it all on his own all the time."

Years later Currie could still vividly remember the game: "I can still see Alastair Robertson putting one of his studs into me and how I didn't break my leg I'll never know. There was a great big hole in my leg the perfect shape of a stud and I went off and got it stitched. He'd gone through my shin-pad and I swore I'd get him back for that."

Despite the attempts to maim Leeds' new golden boy, West Brom's John Wile rated Currie's performance that day as one of the most impressive he had ever seen. "For a class midfield display," the central defender told *Shoot!*, "I must nominate Tony Currie, playing for Leeds United with West Bromwich as the opposition.

"Leeds took a 2-0 lead over us, and Currie was their inspiration. He never put a foot wrong, and although we fought back to level the score nothing could detract from Tony's contribution for United. His natural game is to pick up the ball from his own defenders, then spark off attacks, and this is what he did constantly throughout the 90 minutes. And Currie did everything in that match with style and flair."

Although Leeds made a poor start to the 1976-77 season, winning only one and losing four of their first eight games, Currie's form was soon earning rave reviews.

"Leeds' £240,000 investment in flair, finesse and an eye-catching future," Barry Foster drooled a few games into the season, "is only self-discipline away from being a midfield player regarded among the best soccer has ever produced."

But as Barry Foster noted, even Tony Currie couldn't win games on his own. For all the chances he was creating, Leeds' strikers seemed strangely reluctant to convert them.

With Leeds struggling in front of goal (and with Allan Clarke picking up a serious knee injury in October that would rule him out of action until December), Armfield had no option but to reach for his chequebook, signing burly striker Ray Hankin from Burnley for £172,000. Unfortunately for Leeds and the player, after just four games for his new club, Hankin also suffered a serious knee injury that curtailed his season.

Hankin and Currie would become room-mates and firm friends and often socialised together, which on one occasion got the pair into hot water with their manager.

"Once I had to drag Currie and Hankin, two of my big signings, over the coals when I heard they had been involved in an afternoon drinking session in town," Armfield recalls. "I gave them the biggest rollicking I have ever handed out in my life and finished by saying, 'You have let the club down, you have let me down and you have let yourselves down. And you could have been in serious trouble. If I ever have any problems with either of you again, I'll sell you immediately.' Neither ever gave another moment's trouble."

Meanwhile, back on the pitch inconsistency and a lack of goals ensured Leeds could offer no advance on mid-table mediocrity during Currie's first season at Elland Road. The departures of so many of Revie's luminaries and the advancing years of those who stayed, had inevitably diminished Leeds' potency, particularly at home where attendances dipped on occasion below 20,000, while injuries at key times to key players (including Currie), and the introduction of several inexperienced youngsters made for a constantly changing line-up.

After a second round exit from the League Cup (courtesy of a 2-1 defeat at Stoke City), Leeds' only hopes of winning the silverware that Currie craved rested in the FA Cup. The Whites launched their campaign in spectacular fashion with a 5-2 rout of Norwich City – all five goals coming in a scintillating first half (including one from fit-again Allan Clarke). Victories against Birmingham City, Manchester City and Wolves in successive rounds steered Leeds into the semi-finals and a date with Tommy Docherty's Manchester United. For Currie it was the first time he had reached such a stage in major domestic competition.

In the semi-final at Hillsborough against Manchester United, two early goals rocked Leeds on their heels, and although Clarke pulled a goal back from the penalty spot, it was too little, too late.

Currie, who had come to Leeds to win things, was understandably devastated: "After Manchester United beat us in the 1977 FA Cup semi the atmosphere in the dressing room was just like the aftermath of that Poland game. Don Howe, I think, came in ranting and raving, so someone told him to shut up."

After the semi-final defeat in April, Leeds' season meandered to its conclusion and ultimately finished with the club in a rather desultory tenth place, which, of course, meant that there would be no European football to look forward to – a failure that would have been unthinkable during the Revie era.

In the league, Leeds could only muster 48 goals from 42 games and Joe Jordan's 12 (from all competitions) was the lowest top-scorer's total since the club's formation.

Indeed the one bright spot in an otherwise disappointing season was the form of Tony Currie, who impressed almost everyone with his dribbling and long-range passing ability.

"Tony is almost as accurate as the world's number one passer, Johnny Giles," Leeds skipper Trevor Cherry eulogised. "He can switch play with a pinpoint diagonal pass and his corners and free kicks are perfection."

As far as Armfield was concerned Tony Currie was the best midfielder in the country at that time. "Tony Currie was a great success… He was a tremendous talent, technically gifted, strong and naturally fit. That will come as a surprise to the people who used to knock Tony because he never really looked athletic.

On one occasion, he had been out of action for about four weeks and I pushed him straight back into the side as soon as he was off the treatment table. I was told he should have had a run-out with the reserves or a week's full training but I knew he would be OK. He played the full 90 minutes without a problem. He was hugely popular with the crowd."

"By our standards," Leeds assistant manager Maurice Lindley added at the end of the campaign, "last season wasn't too good for the team. And on top of that, Tony himself had a pretty tough time with injuries. Had he chosen to do so, he could have nursed himself along. But he didn't. He was back in our box, looking for the ball, then straight up the pitch to support the attack. He got through a ton of work."

Although Currie had added to his game the consistency that many people believed had eluded him at Sheffield, Tony could not quite suppress the innate urge to express himself. "No matter how hard I tried," Currie explained, "my instincts led me to let my hair down on the pitch. You know what I mean – I was blowing kisses and waving to the fans, exchanging backchat with them at throw-ins and corners and generally letting them know that I appreciated their presence!

"The fans have paid good money to watch us," Tony continued, "and I believe in making them feel part of the proceedings."

Elland Road's smitten fans reciprocated by voting him their Player of the Year.

For some, though, the jury was still out on Currie. One of his most persistent critics within the Leeds set-up was Eddie Gray, who believed Tony never quite applied himself to the fullest extent of his enormous talent.

"While accepting that no one footballer can be expected to have everything," Gray remarks in his autobiography, "and that the secret of all successful teams lies in their blend of players, I still feel Tony sold himself short. What made this particularly hard to accept was that he was so well built and strong. As someone who got on well with Tony – I liked him immensely as a person – I would often nag him about it. 'You have so much more to give,' I would tell him. 'You have to change the way you think about the game.' He agreed, but old habits die hard."

Currie, for his part, was of the opinion that his principal job was to make the plays, not spend his time concentrating on stopping others doing so. "If I think I should be doing something I'll do it," Currie explained in 1978, "no matter what anybody else thinks. You can go back over the years and find plenty of players who stay out of the game and then come up with a winner. That's my way of playing. If you're being tightly marked it's no good just running all over the pitch getting nowhere. It sometimes pays to stay out of the game for a bit so that you can try to work something out."

Currie was self-assured rather than conceited, a point he has always been keen to stress: "Some of the boys might have thought, 'Who's this big-headed bugger?' – but that wasn't me. I was like that on the field because I knew what I could do.

"I was an introvert off the pitch, but throw a ball at my feet and I switched on. It was my stage. I loved showing people what I could do. Hitting a ball 70 yards and have it land at someone's feet is an art and there's not many people who can do it. I loved doing the long balls, the little chips, the spin backs. There were a lot of hard men around in those days, but it wasn't a case of them targeting me for being fancy. They knew my ability and they knew if they could stop Currie they'd stop Leeds ticking."

* * * * *

Although there were no more high profile departures on the playing side of the staff in the pre-season, there was one notable change behind the scenes when Don Howe left to take up the post as Arsenal first team coach. Currie was not impressed.

"They were naïve in letting him go," Currie believes, "because he and Jimmy Armfield were a great team. Don was the hard man and a very good coach, while Jimmy was the softly spoken manager. They were different personalities but it worked. When Arsenal came in for Don they let him go just like that, which was bloody ridiculous."

Despite these setbacks, the pre-season signing of Aberdeen's industrious winger Arthur Graham and the return to fitness of Ray Hankin were both cause for optimism as the 1977-78 season approached.

Certainly Currie was in a bullish mood. "This time," Tony predicted, "I think we can make that slight improvement which will win us the league or a cup. When I left Sheffield I thought I was moving to a club which would go places – and I haven't changed my opinion."

With Allan Clarke ruled out with injury until February, Armfield twinned Hankin with Joe Jordan and the new-look forward line hit the ground running with Hankin helping himself to nine goals from the opening ten games.

Despite Hankin's early-season form, Leeds got off to a disastrous start to the 1977-78 season, registering only three wins from their opening 12 games. Leeds were scoring plenty of goals; the trouble was they were conceding more.

With his side suffering in 14th place Jimmy Armfield decided the midfield needed bolstering and paid Burnley £175,000 for their diminutive but combative Welshman, Brian Flynn.

"He was only 22 but had played over 100 games for Burnley and had over 20 caps for Wales," Armfield stated. "He wasn't much over 5ft tall but he was very fit, mobile and a good tackler. He could play a bit too, the ideal foil for Currie."

As far as Eddie Gray was concerned, Brian Flynn was bought to do the donkey work that was anathema to Currie: "Tony had as much skill as anyone. I enjoyed playing with him because of his passing ability. I think everybody did.

But while he compared favourably with Billy and John in his technical ability, he lacked their discipline and work ethic. Both Billy and John worked hard off the ball as well as on it. If either lost the ball, he would always try to win it back or prevent his opponent doing whatever he wished with it. Tony's contribution in that department was erratic, which helps explain why Jimmy bought the industrious Brian Flynn from Burnley to complement him."

Although not merely a water-carrier or aggressive ball-winner, Flynn's brio and endeavour gave Currie the freedom to provide the frills and spills that fans paid to see.

"Flynny was great," Currie extols. "He had the lot. He knew his capabilities and we developed a great understanding. He was always looking for me to give me the ball and he was always there to help out if there was trouble."

The feeling was mutual. "Tony was a great talent," Flynn doffs, "who could tease defenders and make a mockery of opponents. On his day he was a joy to play alongside."

Flynn made his debut in the draw with Norwich City on 5th November and his impact on Leeds' fortunes was immediate. With Ray Hankin rediscovering some of his early-season touch in front of goal, Leeds were soon enjoying the fruits of a nine-game unbeaten run. The run, which included consecutive victories against Manchester City, Nottingham Forest, West Ham and QPR, moved them from 12th place to up to sixth in the league.

But just when it seemed like Armfield had manoeuvred Leeds into a strong position, one from which a title challenge could possibly be mounted, three defeats in the four games of the crucial festive period sent Leeds crashing back to the reality of ninth place.

The club was rocked further when its star striker Joe Jordan handed in a transfer request. Although Jordan's stated reasons for leaving were predicated on a desire to play abroad, when a potential move to Ajax fell through, Jordan moved instead to Manchester United for £300,000 – an act of unspeakable treachery in the eyes of Leeds' fans.

In actual fact Jordan had been discontented for some time. "After the [European Cup Final team of 1975] was broken up," Jordan was once quoted as saying, "I thought that was it. I was a bit disillusioned, as a lot of people were. I wanted to try and win things, and I really did not think we were going to do that."

Presciently, the day after Jordan's exit, on 7th January, Leeds crashed out of the FA Cup at the hands of Manchester City, in a bad-tempered third round clash marred by serious crowd trouble prompted by rioting Leeds fans. It was, in the words of Eddie Gray, "One of the blackest days in the club's history."

When Peter Barnes put City 2-0 up in the 72nd minute, visiting keeper Joe Corrigan turned to the Elland Road Kop with his arms raised in celebration.

In the disgraceful scenes that followed, Corrigan was pelted with missiles and then confronted by one lunatic who had somehow eluded security to get onto the pitch. This was the cue for more riotous supporters to take to the field. With hordes of idiots running amok, referee Colin Seel decided to take the players off as mounted police attempted to restore order.

After a delay of 15 minutes order was restored sufficiently to allow the game to restart. Although a Frank Gray penalty pulled a goal back, Leeds were unable to level and force a replay. To compound the misery of being dumped out of the cup, the club would also face severe censure from the FA.

As a result of the shameful crowd disturbances Leeds decided to erect a fence around the Kop but it was not enough to deter the Football Association from clobbering the club with a three-year ban on staging home ties in the FA Cup, although this was later commuted to one year.

The rioting fans were only part of the drama however. During the first half Leeds' keeper David Harvey and Gordon McQueen exchanged punches as United prepared to defend a Manchester City corner, resulting in an embarrassing scuffle.

Perhaps unsurprisingly, the Manchester City game proved to be Gordon McQueen's last for Leeds. Restless without his close friend, Joe Jordan, McQueen also handed in a transfer request and in the blink of an eye was on his way to join his fellow Scottish international at Old Trafford for a then British record fee of £495,000

After crossing the great divide, McQueen burnt yet more bridges by spitefully telling the press that Leeds were going nowhere, claiming the club lacked ambition. Unfortunately for McQueen, Manchester United were also going nowhere, at least while he and Jordan were in their side.

Armfield was devastated to lose the services of such solid performers. "We were on our way to the last four of the League Cup as 1978 began," he maintained. "I felt we were on the brink of real progress."

As far as Eddie Gray was concerned, the sale of Jordan and McQueen were an all too clear indication that the glory days were long gone. "Neither player would have dreamt of making such a move in the Revie days," Gray asserts in his autobiography.

"It was another bad mistake by the club letting them go to Manchester United," Currie agrees, "and I think it was a mistake for them too. I mean they hardly set the world on fire there, did they?"

While significant profits were made on both players, the fact that Leeds had sold two of their best players to one of their fiercest rivals seemed to speak volumes about the club's ambition, confirming Jordan and McQueen's criticisms.

Perversely, the departures of Jordan and McQueen marked the start of a purple run of form, as Leeds rattled off three consecutive victories against Birmingham, Coventry and Ipswich, propelling the club back to sixth place in the league.

Nevertheless, after their third round exit in the FA Cup and with a genuine title challenge unrealistic, the League Cup represented the club's only chance of silverware. After comfortable wins against Rochdale, Colchester United, Bolton Wanderers and Everton, Leeds found themselves in the last four of the competition.

The two-legged semi-final pitched Leeds against their former manager Brian Clough's Nottingham Forest team, who were at that time heading for the First Division title and European immortality the following year. In two distinctly one-sided affairs, Leeds found themselves on the receiving end of a 7-3 aggregate mauling.

Although Leeds quickly regrouped with a 2-0 win against Chelsea (Frank Gray and Currie scoring the goals), and a tremendous 1-0 win over Manchester United (Allan Clarke at last returning from injury to net the winner), Leeds stretched their winning streak in the league to five. With almost a third of the season remaining, a European place seemed tantalisingly within reach.

Disappointingly all hopes of European football evaporated as Leeds won only one of their last seven games, a run that saw them slump to another profoundly mediocre ninth place finish. After two seasons at Elland Road, in which he had made 70 league appearances, Currie was disappointed to note that he had only scored four league goals.

"I honestly don't know what went wrong," Tony explained. "I was inhibited by a foot injury. Every time I whacked the ball I found I was in pain for the rest of the game so I tended not to try long distance efforts. And as I was playing deeper than usual in midfield for long periods I wasn't getting much chance near goal." Tony's solution was simple (and illustrative of his commitment to the cause), heading to Elland Road at least three times a week over the summer to practise his shooting.

In the pre-season two more Revie legends called time on their Elland Road careers. Allan Clarke left to take over as player-manager at Barnsley while Paul Reaney, a veteran of over 700 first team appearances for Leeds, moved to Bradford City on a free. To replace Clarke, Armfield had bought Hull City goal poacher John Hawley for £81,000 to partner Ray Hankin in attack.

Although Leeds had allowed their manager to carry on rebuilding by authorising his purchase of Hawley, in actual fact, Armfield was living on borrowed time.

Armfield had guided the club to a European Cup Final, and to the semi-finals of the FA Cup and the League Cup in consecutive seasons. Furthermore, by common consent most of Armfield's signings had been shrewd ones and he had tackled the delicate but unavoidable task of incrementally dismantling Revie's ageing side with considerable aplomb.

Unfortunately for Armfield, his achievements were ultimately not sufficient to satisfy the Leeds United board and supporters who were impatient for a return to the success on which they had gorged under Revie and with the 1978-79 season just over a month away, Armfield was relieved of his duties.

"To be honest, I think he would have gone earlier if it hadn't been for some of the players," Currie claims. "We saved his job for a number of months. A few of us had a word with the chairman and said, 'Come on, give him a bit longer.'"

When the bell finally tolled for Armfield, Currie was sorry to see him go: "I loved Jimmy, but I don't think many players at Leeds had as much respect for him as they should have done. Maybe it was because he was coming in on the back of Revie. But I thought Jimmy and Don [Howe] were a good partnership, and Jimmy did buy the likes of me, Ray Hankin and Brian Flynn.

"He made us an attractive side. But we didn't achieve success under him. We were short of perhaps two quality players who would have enabled us to compete more favourably."

While there were many Leeds fans that felt he was on the right path, others believed the amiable, mild-mannered Armfield lacked the ruthlessness and decisiveness necessary to succeed in top management. Perhaps Armfield suspected as much himself. The Leeds hot seat turned out to be his last managerial post and Armfield turned instead to a career as a respected journalist and radio commentator.

8

1978–79

*"I don't feel I let anyone down in
my time at Leeds."*

– Tony Currie

IT says much for Leeds' declining prestige that none
of the candidates lined up to replace Jimmy Armfield
– reportedly Southampton boss Lawrie McMenemy,
Sheffield Wednesday supremo Jack Charlton and Arsenal
coach Don Howe – could be tempted away from their
posts.

With faithful retainer Maurice Lindley in caretaker
charge until a new manager could be found let alone
appointed, Leeds and Currie got their 1978-79 campaign
off to a promising start with a 2-2 draw away at Arsenal.

The game was billed as a midfield face-off between
the teams' respective magicians, Liam Brady and Tony
Currie. On the sunbathed, manicured Highbury pitch
the Englishman drew first blood with an exquisite strike
from an almost impossible angle near the goal line; a goal
of such jaw-dropping awesomeness it even drew gasps

and applause from the Gunners faithful. No less of an authority than Bobby Charlton once described the goal as the best he'd ever seen, which is some compliment.

Amazingly Currie had hinted to the press that they could expect something special, having been inspired, he said, by "some of the breathtaking shooting in the World Cup."

Brady drew the Gunners level from the spot before half-time then put his side ahead shortly after the break with a stunning 20-yard shot with the outside of his famed left peg. Currie, though, was not to be outshone and ensured his side shared the spoils when he set up a late equaliser for Trevor Cherry after a deft run and cross down the left.

By the next game, at home to Manchester United, Leeds had their new man in charge: legendary Celtic boss Jock Stein, at that time the most successful club manager in the history of the British game, having guided Celtic to nine consecutive Scottish League titles between 1966 and 1974, a trophy cabinet full of other domestic honours, and, lest we forget, that immortal European Cup victory in 1967.

By 1978, however, there were those who believed that, as a result of injuries sustained in a serious car crash in 1975 (that almost cost Stein his life) as well as heart problems, Stein's powers were on the wane.

While the fact that Rangers won the Scottish League title in 1976 (during Stein's convalescent leave), and the fact that Celtic won it back in 1977 (following Stein's recovery and return) could have been more fairly interpreted as further evidence of Stein's greatness; when Rangers wrestled the title back in 1978, those in the Celtic boardroom who were less disposed towards Stein decided it was time to relieve him of his first team duties.

In the summer of 1978 Stein, against his will, was pushed upstairs (to take up a vague general manager role) to make way for new Parkhead manager, his former captain Billy McNeill.

Believing he still had a great deal to offer as a "tracksuit manager", Stein was insulted when he discovered that his new role would involve little more than running Celtic's Pools competition, and, stung by being told by the Celtic board that he was, in essence, washed up as a football manager at the age of 55, Stein was desperate for a new challenge.

"I did not want to stay at Celtic as a director," he later explained. "I feel I have too much to offer football and I wanted closer involvement."

Although Stein was being strongly tipped to become Scotland's next manager should Ally McLeod be relieved of his duties, as was likely, following Scotland's disastrous 1978 World Cup campaign in Argentina, when the offer came to manage Leeds, Stein, on 21st August, accepted the post. Stein later admitted his acceptance of the position had been hasty.

Although the new manager's first game ended in a 3-2 defeat, Stein's next two games in charge both resulted in impressive 3-0 wins, first at home against Wolves and then away at Chelsea.

Stein's presence initially galvanised the entire club – players and fans alike. "For the first time since Don Revie walked out," wrote the local *Evening Post*, "Elland Road was fizzing with that unique atmosphere particular to a top soccer club. Gone was the cathedral-like quiet, the air of apparent disinterest."

What was not "particular to a top soccer club", however, was the fact that Stein had inherited a squad that was, in all truth, paper thin on top quality football players. One player that the new gaffer did like the look of, however, was Currie, and during his short period in charge Stein referred in glowing terms to the man around whom he intended to build the team. Stein even entrusted Tony with the captain's armband – a decision that raised more than a few eyebrows in the media.

The Leeds assistant manager however insisted that the leopard had changed his spots, and believed that the players would respond better to Currie than they did to the previous skipper, Trevor Cherry. "Tony has proved in the close season that he could captain any side," Maurice Lindley informed *The Daily Telegraph*. "He's not swayed by emotion from anybody, and he can command and demand from any player, which is the answer in this game... [The lazy image is] the past. There's a different man now. I don't know the turning point, but his work rate has improved, and confidence oozes out of him. He's also disciplined himself to be less spectacular. Perhaps, too, it has to do with coming to a club with internationals all around; brings you down to earth; from being god of one you become one of the many."

Unfortunately, Currie picked up a leg strain only three league games into Stein's reign and missed most of the one full month – September 1978 – that the former Celtic man was in charge at Elland Road. It is worth noting that Stein was surprised and impressed to learn Currie remained determined to play despite his injury.

Currie's worth to Leeds was never better illustrated than by his latest injury setback. Tony had left the club in a promising fifth place after the Chelsea game. By the time he had returned after an absence of five league games the club had plummeted to 13th!

Without the services of their star player, Stein's Leeds succumbed to defeats away at Manchester City and at home to Tottenham and drew away at Coventry. Despite a win at home to Birmingham, it was becoming clear to Stein that the task of restoring Leeds to former glories was going to be an arduous one.

With his wife, Jean, back in Glasgow, having elected not to follow her husband south of the border, and having seen all attempts to bolster his squad come to nought, Stein rapidly became disheartened and disillusioned.

Stein was handed an escape route out of Elland Road when the Scotland job finally became available following Ally McLeod's inevitable dismissal. Although Stein was the obvious candidate as successor, the fact that he was now the manager of Leeds initially seemed to rule him out of the Scottish Football Association's considerations.

If he wanted another crack at the Scotland job, Stein knew that he had to tunnel out of Elland Road quickly. After a lifetime of wrapping the Scottish media around his little finger, the canny Stein had soon devised his plan – telephoning BBC correspondent and long-time confidante, Archie MacPherson and encouraging him to drop strong hints on the BBC's *Sportsnight* programme that he was available. Stein himself meanwhile would maintain in public an "I'm-content-at-Leeds" neutrality.

"Tell London that you can say something about the Scotland job and me," Stein told the reporter. "You could go on and say something to the effect that you believe I would be interested in going back to Scotland. You know how to phrase these things. You can't say you've been talking to me. Just play it like you're confident that I would take the job. Make it sound like the SFA are being a bit slow on this."

MacPherson obliged, telling Harry Carpenter that all the SFA had to do was pick up the telephone and contact the Big Man and he would be Scotland's next boss.

Apparently, MacPherson was not the only journalist Stein had press-ganged into his service, and in less time than it takes Scotland to get dumped out of a major tournament, the lobbying to appoint Stein had proved irresistible. Despite the best efforts of Manny Cussins to persuade Stein to stay, on 4th October, just 45 days after joining Leeds, Stein was offered and accepted the Scotland post.

Although it would be hard to begrudge Stein's desire to return home to his wife and the irresistible challenge of riding to his country's rescue, there were several cynics in the Leeds dressing room who felt upset and resentful at both the manner and the abruptness of Stein's departure; believing he had used Leeds to force the SFA's hand.

Currie was among them: "I thought what Jock Stein did was disgraceful. To come in and use a club like Leeds as a stepping-stone was shocking. I mean, his name was being bandied about and it was obvious he was going to get the Scottish job. I thought what he did was wrong, but he didn't have a job at the time because he had retired from Celtic and he didn't want to be out of work.

"As a man he was fine. He loved me and he was one of the old-style managers that talked to individuals more than he did the whole team. He was very similar to Shankly although Bill was a lot more outrageous and outgoing, and John Harris at Sheffield had the same sort of Scottish calm."

With Maurice Lindley yet again placed in temporary charge, Leeds United's first game following Stein's departure was a League Cup third round meeting at Bramall Lane with Sheffield United, surprise winners against Liverpool in round two. Tony was understandably desperate to play, but faced a race against the clock to be fit in time.

Fortunately the European commitments of Leeds' second round opponents, West Brom, necessitated the late staging of the two second round replays it took for Leeds to emerge victorious. As a result Leeds' third round tie was also pushed back, allowing Currie the extra time he needed to recover from his thigh strain. Had the tie been played as scheduled, Currie would have certainly missed out on the sentimental return to the Lane he craved.

In the event, when the match did take place – on 10th October – Currie was still only half-fit and had to lie about his fitness to secure his selection.

Prior to the game, Sheffield United manager Harry Haslam predicted a warm welcome for the former Bramall Lane idol: "People here still remember Tony, of course, for all the good things he gave them. We are happy to see he is fit again, but he will get the respect of fellow professionals rather than hero worship when he steps on to the field. Nobody is going to back down because of his reputation, but I'm sure the crowd will receive him well. After all, he is the sort of player who pleases crowds."

In the event, although Leeds strolled to a comfortable 4-1 win, with Tony observing the indomitable "law of the ex" by scoring one of the goals, the night was not an entirely happy one for the former Blade.

With the score at 2-0 chants of "Currie is a fat twat" echoed around the Kop. Although Currie's response – jovially lifting his jersey to show off his trimmest ever physique – suggested he could roll with the crowd's punches, behind the banter Currie was devastated to be the target of such abuse from those to whom he had given so much. "They'd loved me for eight and a half years and I loved them," he lamented. "It hurt."

While United's visit to Sheffield set new record gate receipts for the Bramall Lane ground with a crowd of

40,899 paying £60,003 to witness / taunt Currie's return, the former Blades idol at least had the satisfaction of the last laugh: "That result at Bramall Lane was very special, I was the subject of non-stop abuse down there and to win 4-1 and score as well was fantastic."

Incidentally, when *The Green 'Un* (South Yorkshire's Saturday evening football paper) was published the following weekend, its letters page was plastered with complaints from those who had been disgusted by the way their former hero had been maltreated. One such letter came from the Blades' promotions manager, Mick Rooker, who wrote, "I could not understand why people would want to get at someone who had been such a great servant to the Club. It was out of order."

Touched by Rooker's heartfelt loyalty, Currie wrote a letter of thanks and enclosed a signed picture.

As Leeds' form in the league dipped, the need to appoint a new manager became an urgent matter. In the event, Leeds turned to eccentric, pipe-chewing Sunderland gaffer, Jimmy Adamson. Adamson was at that time one of the most widely respected figures in the game. Although never capped by England, Adamson had won the Footballer of the Year award in 1962 whilst captain of Burnley and had been assistant manager to Walter Winterbottom during the World Cup in Chile, while still a player himself. Indeed, when Winterbottom resigned as England's manager in 1962, the FA offered Adamson the post. Adamson, however, decided to turn down the offer, believing he lacked the necessary experience. Following his retirement as a player in 1964, Adamson joined the Burnley coaching staff, eventually becoming the Clarets' manager in 1970.

With former Burnley defender Dave Merrington as his assistant, Adamson managed Burnley, with some success, for six years between 1970 and 1976, and had been in charge of Sunderland, again with Merrington by his side, for two years when the Elland Road position lured him away from Roker Park.

Although Adamson's stature within the game commanded respect, the players who worked with him recall his endearing reputation for occasionally indecipherable team-talks.

"Jimmy was all right, but he was an oddball," Currie later remarked. "I had a lot respect for him, but he was pretty strange. The way he spoke was baffling. You had to listen very carefully to work out what he was talking about. He'd say something and mean another. It was like a bloody riddle. But when I did eventually decipher what he was saying, I thought it was actually quite good."

Despite his reputation as a tracksuit manager, Adamson, Eddie Gray believes, took too much of a back seat during the week, and seemed content to cede a great deal of the training ground responsibilities to the man he had brought with him from Sunderland to be his assistant at Elland Road – Dave Merrington.

"This led to some confusion," Gray notes in his autobiography. "The way Merrington got us to play in training did not always tie in with Adamson's instructions to us before a match on the Saturday. It does seem strange that this should have happened, bearing in mind that the pair knew each other so well."

It is fair to say that Currie was not a Merrington fan. "[He was] an unbelievable bloke," Tony elaborates. "He was one of them that would throw tea-cups and go mad. One day in the dressing room at half-time he was giving the lads a right going over and I looked at Hank and took the mickey behind his back. On the Monday I found I'd been stitched up by the youth team coach who'd seen me do it. Merrington got hold of me and shoved me up against the wall. He's a big chap and he's my coach, so I'm not going to do anything because it would get me in lumber. He threatened me and said, 'If you ever do that again I'll do you.' I just looked at him and said absolutely nothing. He was a nutcase and the players all thought so. He was very conscientious and had his own ideas, but the bloke was a bloody idiot."

"I have to admit that Merrington was not someone I enjoyed working with," Eddie Gray agrees. "His personality could best be described as high-octane. He was a strong-minded character who seemed to see things in black and white and I felt he wanted you to do things his way or not at all. I took exception to the manner in which I felt he tried to impose his beliefs upon people. They included his belief as a born-again Christian. One day he called a meeting of the players in one of the Elland Road bars.

"Two towering athletes introduced to us as leading American football players endeavoured to give us what I interpreted as a lecture on how the Bible and Jesus had helped them achieve success. There might well have been a lot more to it but I did not hang around to find out. I just told Merrington that this line of approach to my job as a professional footballer was not for me, and with one or two of the other players, I got up and left."

Despite the players' reservations about Merrington, Adamson's appointment initially seemed a good one with the new man guiding a rejuvenated Leeds to another League Cup semi-final and an astonishing 16-match unbeaten run in the league that lasted from the draw with Wolves on 18th November until the 4-1 reverse at Manchester United on 24th March. Inevitably, the prime architect of Leeds' revival was Tony Currie, revelling in the responsibility of captaincy and adding a maturity to his extravagant gifts.

Currie, who, with Flynn, was the only outfield player to appear in all 16 of the unbeaten fixtures, was playing some of the finest football of his entire career: "Jimmy Adamson once said to me," Currie details, "'a player with your class and skill should never fall below 80 per cent in any game you play.' I knew exactly what he meant and told him not to worry."

Although Currie had only scored four league goals in his first two seasons at Leeds, the first half of the 1978-79 campaign saw Currie notch seven goals, including an absolute beauty in the 4-0 win against Southampton on 25th November.

Tony Currie had been in majestic form all afternoon against the Saints, and his goal ten minutes into the second half was the icing on the cake of a complete all-round performance.

When Currie robbed Baker of possession 25 yards from goal little seemed on, with Chris Nicholl blocking Tony's route to goal and Gennoe, Southampton's keeper, well placed. With a minimum of backlift and effort, Currie confounded science and the Southampton defence to bend a 25-yard banana shot that curved in a sumptuous arc to land in the only spot that was guaranteed to beat the flailing Gennoe. It was a breathtaking goal that drew rapturous applause from the fans behind the goal at the Gelderd End. "Oh, my goodness!" ejaculated Martin Tyler whilst commentating for Yorkshire Television, "... and Tony Currie milks the applause that is so deserved."

Few players would have attempted such audacity let alone pulled it off. It was, without a shadow of a doubt, a goal to rank among the best of Currie's career and was later voted ITV's *Big Match* Goal of the Season for 1978-79.

"I've always liked scoring goals," Currie said, "and when I was at Sheffield I used to reckon on nine or ten a season. Before this season I'd struggled with goals at Leeds but I used to have trouble with a hamstring and was always a little bit worried about getting full power in my shooting. Now I've got my confidence back and I'm hoping there will be a few more over the rest of the season like the one I got against Southampton."

For a brief spell, Leeds United were sitting in fourth place and with a second successive League Cup semi approaching, seemed on the verge of actually winning something. Alas it was not to be.

Having faced the mighty Red Devils of Manchester and the league champions elect Nottingham Forest in their previous two semi-final outings, their League Cup opponents this time around – Southampton – appeared to offer a much more realistic chance of a Wembley date.

Indeed, after drubbing the Saints 4-0 earlier in the season, Leeds were hot favourites to progress. In the first leg at Elland Road, Leeds built a two-nil lead with goals from Currie and Ray Hankin and seemed to be cruising towards Wembley. However with just 20 minutes to go, the Saints, captained by Currie's old friend, rival and adversary Alan Ball, staged a late fightback to draw level. In hindsight, the 1-0 second leg defeat at The Dell, which sent the Hampshire club through to their second Wembley final in three years, seemed almost inevitable. "I was getting used to it," Currie recalls wistfully.

A third semi-final defeat in as many years was a shattering blow to Currie. "It's a really awful feeling to lose in a semi-final," Tony told the official *Leeds United Magazine* in February 1996, "I was only at Elland road for three seasons and we lost one each year. But the two in the

League Cup were particularly difficult to accept because we were basically responsible for our own downfall."

Currie must have realised that the chances of decorating his career with some silverware were now decreasing by the year. Certainly there seemed little chance of a decent FA Cup run for Leeds in 1979, thanks to the ban on staging home ties they'd received the previous season. Having seen off Hartlepool at the Victoria Ground in the third round, Leeds were drawn "at home" to West Brom. Although Leeds shared six goals when the original tie was played at the Hawthorns, in the replay, also held at the Hawthorns, United fell to a 2-0 extra-time defeat and crashed out of the cup.

Leeds' only hope of securing European football, therefore, rested on a top six finish in the league. Despite a 4-1 loss at Man United, and three winless fixtures against Southampton, Ipswich and Middlesbrough, 1-0 wins against Aston Villa and Everton (Currie scoring the winner in the latter – his last goal for Leeds), a 5-1 trouncing of Bolton Wanderers and a 4-3 triumph against QPR, secured the necessary points to earn Leeds a respectable fifth place finish and a place in the UEFA Cup.

Sadly, Currie would not be around to share it, when at the end of the 1978-79 season he abruptly handed in a transfer request. The reason behind this unexpected development was due entirely to his wife Linda's health problems. Homesick and unable to settle in Leeds, coupled with a long-standing problem with nerves and depression, Linda yearned to move back to London. For the sake of his marriage, Tony decided that a transfer to a London club was the only solution and reluctantly requested a transfer.

"Life was becoming unbearable at Leeds," Currie told *Shoot!* magazine. "Not, I hasten to add, because of the club or the fans. They were both great, but simply because my wife, who comes from London and loves the place as much as I do, was getting very depressed.

"Linda suffered from depression when we were in Sheffield, especially when the club weren't doing well and it took its toll on me. She wanted to go back to London then and although things improved for a year or two when we went to Leeds they got progressively worse after that. I went to London to fetch her back a couple of times and in the end I said I would ask Jimmy Adamson for a transfer."

Adamson knew that such a move would not only prove unpopular with the Leeds faithful, it would also seriously diminish his chances of restoring former glories to Elland Road, and, by association, his own chances of keeping his job.

"Poor sod," Currie sympathised. "When I told him he poured himself a whisky and said, 'They'll lynch me.' Then he asked me if I wanted one, but I said I'd better not. I walked out and he might have been drinking all day after that. I knew how he felt. It broke my bloody heart to leave Leeds."

"I would have stayed at Elland Road," Currie stated on another occasion. "We were playing some good stuff and I had a great relationship with the crowd. I only left for family reasons."

Currie's transfer request was reluctantly accepted. "It is not a question of the board considering his request," Manny Cussins told the press. "We cannot keep him and he is now up for sale."

At first Leeds put a £600,000 price tag on their playmaker – which seemed to deter the two clubs purportedly heading the queue for Tony's services – Watford, newly promoted to the Second Division, and First Division Brighton and Hove Albion – neither of whom could afford such a fee for a 29-year-old.

To accelerate matters, Leeds even slashed their original asking price to £400,000, but it seems that unbeknownst to Tony at the time, behind the scenes the Leeds board had no intention of selling Tony to any of their First Division rivals.

"I found out afterwards that a few other First Division clubs were after me at that time," Tony later revealed, "but Leeds didn't want me to go to another First Division club. But I found out that Arsenal and Spurs were both interested in me." In the event, it was Second Division Queens Park Rangers (who needed someone to fill the breach caused by the departure of their captain Gerry Francis to Crystal Palace), who won the race for Currie's signature. Following talks with QPR boss Tommy Docherty and Hoops chairman Jim Gregory, on 10th August 1979, Currie put pen to paper. The £400,000 fee was for QPR then a club record.

Given that Currie was by universal consent playing some of the best football of his career and was arguably approaching his prime, Tony was laying a lot on the line by dropping down a league. What's more, because *he* requested the move, Currie would forfeit his share of the transfer fee, as well as top-flight *and* European football. It was, all things considered, a tremendous sacrifice.

After 124 games and 16 goals Currie's happy three years in West Yorkshire were over (Tony once told me he might have scored more for Leeds but it had often been impossible to prise the ball away from Peter Lorimer when it came to dead ball situations).

Not surprisingly the club's decision to let arguably its most prized asset move on prompted a mixture of grief and hostility from the Elland Road faithful.

"We have not sold Currie just for the sake of making money," Manny Cussins stated in an attempt to placate the fans. "We did not want to sell him and have only done so under pressure from the player and under protest."

"Our hand was forced," added Cussins. "His wife had made it clear that she wanted to go back to London and indeed has since done so. This left Currie up here on his own and he has been broken-hearted. He was quite happy with Leeds, but because of his domestic situation sought a move to a London club."

"We are very disappointed," Jimmy Adamson sobbed. "We know he is a crowd puller and a good player, but you have to be compassionate and he wanted to move back to London because of his domestic situation."

In an effort to rationalise the reasons behind her husband's move south, Linda Currie also went public: "I never really liked it in Leeds from the start," she said. "I could not make friends and could not settle. You have to put up with gossip when you are in the public eye, but there were all sorts of things going round. There were stories about wife-swapping and us splitting up and people were quite nasty. I put it down to jealousy. Rumours about Tony being a heavy drinker and it affecting his game and our marriage breaking down were all untrue. Every footballer has a tipple on a Saturday after a match. Tony didn't want to leave Leeds; he was loyal to the club. People who know that wonder why he left, but what they can't seem to understand is that he loves his wife and children more than football and he left for us."

To this day, Tony strenuously denies the rumours that surrounded his departure from Leeds: "I don't know anything about a drink problem or the other stories, but I can assure you they are nonsense. I left for my wife's sake. She had an illness and my football and our life were under strain." Currie, though, has never tried to hide his bitterness at leaving Leeds: "I had a great time at the club and leaving wasn't my fault," he says. "I regret it, but there was nothing I could do about it. Even though I asked for the move I thought they let me go too easy. Why didn't they say, "I know you've got to go back to London, but come up two days a week"? People do that now. Clubs bend over backwards for their players, but I wasn't given any alternative. I went and I was the main schemer. We had a very good team at that point. We had Frankie Gray, Arthur Graham, Hank, Carl Harris, Paul Hart, myself and Flynny. Cor dear. I just don't understand why they did not try to hang on to me. After that season they had a bad year and it was a decade before they replaced me. They bought Alex Sabella, but he was a waste of time: fancy, but not a team man. Not until they got Gary McAllister did they finally get a quality replacement for me. They could have given me some options, but I didn't get one. Not one. It's a shame because that team might have done something."

Instead, three years later, having failed to adequately fill the void Currie had left behind, Leeds were relegated to Division Two, where they would remain until 1990.

Over 20 years after his departure, the fact that Leeds were no more than an average mid-table team during his three years at Elland Road still rankles with Currie; his frustration as keen as it was in 1979.

"Leeds were still a big club when I joined," Currie notes, "but John [Giles] had gone and the others were all in their 30s and on their way out. I only played four games with Billy Bremner, which was a shame, and just one season with Allan Clarke, who was one of the best ever strikers. But they had some good younger players like Joey Jordan and Gordon McQueen and maybe it would have been different if they'd stayed.

"I actually cut out a lot of the showmanship at Leeds, because I wanted to win things. At Sheffield we never had the squad to achieve that, but at Leeds we came close. In my three years there I became a much better player, because when you've got better players around you they drag you up higher. They all wanted to be winners and I wanted to be the best of them."

9

England Comeback

"I know what people say about me – that I'm a showman who is lazy and inconsistent. I mean to prove that those charges are just not true. Maybe my style gives the impression that I'm not doing all I can, but I reckon I'm in the game pretty well all the time – picking up the ball deep, going at defenders and laying off long and short passes."

– Tony Currie

W
HEN Don Revie's reign as England manager came to an unsavoury end, the FA turned to West Ham United's general manager, Ron Greenwood.

Greenwood had long been one of the most respected tacticians in the game, having built the Hammers into a successful team that was widely recognised for playing attractive football and, of course, for nurturing the talents of World Cup winners Geoff Hurst, Martin Peters and Bobby Moore. In contrast with Don Revie, Greenwood encouraged his players to both enjoy and express themselves, urged them to play their natural games and concentrated on tactical simplicity.

Although Greenwood's appointment ultimately came too late to rescue England's bid to qualify for the 1978 World Cup (although he did inspire the team to an impressive 2-0 win against Italy at Wembley), there were several in the media who believed the new coach would put the smile back on the face of both the English team and its supporters, by recalling the flair players who had been so unfairly ignored by his predecessor. Naturally that included Tony Currie.

"Ron Greenwood wasn't everybody's choice as England's manager," posited *Football Monthly* magazine. "But his appointment could provide the national team with a welcome bonus – the fulfilled talents of Tony Currie. Greenwood's reputation as an advocate of the importance of midfield skill provided a new motivation for Currie, who has been in the international background for three years."

Despite years in the wilderness, Currie's thirst for international football remained undimmed and he was understandably itching for another chance to prove himself at the highest level.

"Playing for England means everything to me," Currie emphasised. "I want to get involved with the team again. Sitting at home watching them on TV is no good.

"I'm playing on the left side of midfield now, and I reckon I'm as good as anybody in the country there at the moment. I'd certainly back myself against the others around – Butch Wilkins, Trevor Brooking and Ray Kennedy."

One man who was convinced that Tony should be back in the England fold was Leeds boss, Jimmy Armfield, who even went so far as to telephone Greenwood to tell him that his playmaker was the best midfield player in the country and urged him to consider him – a far cry from today's climate where most Premier League managers would prefer their players *not* to play for their countries.

Although Currie missed out on Greenwood's first four England squads, a telephone call from the new England boss reassured the player that he was part of his plans. "He has already had a chat with me," Currie revealed in February 1978, "and asked me to do things a bit quicker."

One of Greenwood's first tasks as England manager was to re-introduce the 'B' international after an absence from the fixture list of 21 years.

The first such fixture lined up, scheduled for 21st February in Augsburg, was a match against West Germany B. Greenwood was obviously keen to use the fixture to look at a few new and younger faces as well as those unfairly discarded or largely ignored by his predecessor. Greenwood was particularly keen to have a look at Charlie George, Derby County's gifted but mercurial attacker whose international career had hitherto comprised the first 57 minutes of a meaningless friendly against the Republic of Ireland in 1976.

However, when the call-up for the England B team came, George was incandescent at the perceived slap in the face and publicly and petulantly threw it back in the England manager's face.

"Why should I, at 27 years of age, have to travel with an England reserve side?" Charlie complained vociferously in the *Sunday Mirror*: "Why should I have to prove what I can do?"

George's pride opened the door for Currie to take his place in the squad. Currie readily accepted. Unlike Charlie George, Currie evidently preferred to see the glass as half full and regarded the B call-up as an excellent opportunity to play his way back into first team contention. "I didn't intend to finish up as just another star who didn't quite make it," Currie told *Football Monthly*. "I wanted to be acknowledged as a great player – the icing on the cake. And that means being an England regular. I've been aiming at the top since I was at school in Hendon."

Although Tony did not actually feature in England's 2-1 win, his willingness to participate did lead to a recall to the full side in April – against the mighty Brazil.

When the call came, Currie couldn't resist a pointed dig at the previous regime, expressing his resentment at having been so overlooked in favour of more pedestrian "talents": "I believe I'm a naturally gifted player – if that doesn't sound immodest," Currie remarked. "But over the years I've been left out of the England side in favour of donkeys in terms of vision and football skill.

"I believe that brains will beat brawn in time and I'm relieved that at last we have a man in charge who believes that skill, flair and imagination are the key qualities in a professional footballer."

The game with Brazil, whose side included legends like Rivelino (with whom Tony shares his birthday), Cerezo and Zico, should have provided Currie with the perfect setting to prove that he could match the best. Unfortunately, although Gil's goal had put the Brazilians ahead after ten minutes, for the remainder of the match, rather than treating the 92,500-strong crowd, and the England team for that matter, to a footballing exhibition, the South Americans opted instead for a master class in the darker footballing arts. In fact, several Brazilians, Cerezo and full-back Edinho in particular, seemed intent on spoiling the game altogether, with a series of premeditated X-rated challenges. By the end of the match five Brazilians had seen yellow, though a less lenient referee than the Dutch official Charles Corver (the same umpire who ineptly turned a blind eye when West Germany's Harald 'Toni' Schumacher almost decapitated France's Patrick Battiston in the semi-final of the 1982 World Cup) may have shown red on at least a couple of occasions.

For the majority of the match, therefore, it was England and Currie, Barnes and Coppell in particular that resembled classy Latinos and not their South American counterparts. Currie in particular seemed to be enjoying himself immensely, beating his man time and time again and spraying the ball around with his usual elegance and panache. England nevertheless missed plenty of chances to equalise, with Latchford and Francis both spurning gilt-edged chances in the first half that they really ought to have buried.

Although England had a couple of reasonable penalty shouts turned down and had a Cerezo own-goal ruled out following a foul by Latchford, it was not until a well-struck Kevin Keegan free-kick restored parity in the 70th minute and ultimately earned England a well-deserved draw.

Despite a creditable performance and result against one of the favourites to win the 1978 World Cup Greenwood was afterwards privately disappointed that the opposition had not come to play as everyone knew they could: "I would much rather have been beaten by a Brazil team playing the sort of skilled football that is their tradition than holding to a draw a side that, let's be honest, was thuggish in their approach. It was very sad to see them resorting to such tactics. That is not the Brazil way."

Although frustrated by the uncompromising tactics of the opposition, the England manager felt his decision to recall Tony had been more than vindicated. "Tony showed skill and composure and controlled the game," Greenwood raved. "It wasn't an easy baptism because, for most of the time, we took the risk of letting Brazil outnumber us in midfield... but he screened the ball with all the strength of the Brazilians... He outdid the Brazilians in both strength and flair."

Brazil's manager, Claudio Coutinho, was also stirred: "His craftsmanship was superb. I wonder why we haven't heard more of this man."

Currie, quite rightly, was delighted with his contribution, and later rated it as one of the highlights of his career: "I was proud to be a member of an England side that had matched – and often bettered – some of the best players in the world for pure skill."

Currie's performance against the Brazilians ensured that he kept his place in the squad for the next match four weeks later in the Home Championship encounter with Wales at Ninian Park.

Although initially named on the substitutes' bench, Currie was called into action as early as the 16th minute when Trevor Cherry, his Leeds team-mate, was carried off with a fractured collarbone.

With the scores level at 1-1 and the home side pushing for a winner, Currie stepped in to break Welsh hearts.

Picking up a Trevor Francis stab-back on the halfway line, Currie exchanged a short one-two with Steve Coppell before waltzing gracefully infield towards the edge of the Welsh box and unleashing an unstoppable, dipping, swerving, left-foot drive into the top left-hand corner of Dai Davies's goal. Once again John Motson was there to summarise both the action and the scorer with one well-chosen *bon mot*: "Right out of the blue by Tony Currie."

Although Peter Barnes added a late third it was Currie's goal that had effectively settled the contest. His blistering long-range goal, Welsh manager Mike Smith drooled, had been "special enough to win a game anywhere in the world."

As reward, Currie was given a starting berth in the Home International games against Northern Ireland and Scotland at Hampden Park. Both resulted in 1-0 wins for the English, to complete an impressive clean sweep of victories (the first English "triple crown" since 1969) to win the tournament outright for the 31st time.

After only one defeat in his first eight games (against the reigning world champions West Germany in February), it was increasingly evident that Greenwood's appointment had been a good one.

While Revie, with his dossiers and rigid tactical dogma, had filled his players' heads with too much information, Greenwood adopted a more simple approach, one that allowed his players the freedom to express themselves. Additionally, whereas Revie had often selected defenders to play in midfield, with containment and caution the objective, Greenwood's selection placed the emphasis firmly on attack.

Not for Greenwood the midfield destroyer. Instead his bold re-introduction of old-fashioned wingers in the shape of Steve Coppell and Peter Barnes and preference for creative midfielders who were comfortable in possession, like Currie, represented a significant statement of intent and his convictions were vindicated by some highly entertaining displays filled with verve and a number of impressive results. Certainly Tony Currie was impressed.

"Now England have a manager who believes in skill first and strength second," Currie observed, comparing Greenwood favourably to his much-vilified predecessor. "Obviously work-rate is important, too, and despite being labelled lazy and inconsistent I think I do more than my share of work. It means they don't appreciate the amount of thought that goes into my game. Maybe that's the result of my clowning. It probably gives them the impression that I'm not taking the game seriously. But I think a lot about football. I analyse every game – and I try to learn from my mistakes. But one thing I'm dead against is dossiers. Don Revie often used to fill his players' heads with useless information. Ron Greenwood will give individual tips on your opposition, but generally he sends you out with a clear head, and that gives you confidence. It's a terrific morale-booster to know that the manager has faith in you. If a boss treats you like an adult it gives you a greater sense of responsibility. And when he tells you to go out and enjoy yourselves, as Ron Greenwood does, pointing out that you can take the credit while he'll take the blame, it relieves players of a lot of pressure. I think too much attention can be paid to pre-planned tactics. Once out on the park footballers have to be prepared to improvise for the simple reason that you really don't know what the opposition will do."

Greenwood's approach reaped particular dividends in England's next match, a friendly against old foes Hungary. Although Currie would initially have to settle for a place on the bench, he would have had a great vantage point from which to watch England, and Keegan and Brooking in particular, tear the Hungarian defence apart, racing to a 3-0 half-time lead in the process. Although the Magyars pulled a goal back after the break, Currie once again came off the bench to restore England's three-goal advantage with another trademark pile driver from the edge of the Hungarian box.

After five games and two stunning goals following his England comeback, there were many urging Greenwood to give Currie a prolonged run in the national side. "No man in Britain, perhaps in the world," trumpeted *The Telegraph* after the Hungary match in October 1978, "hits a diagonal pass with greater accuracy or less effort; few could have scored the twenty-yard goals that Currie did coming on as a sub against Wales and Hungary."

"He has got everything England needs – skill, stamina and pace," Jimmy Armfield added, no longer the Leeds manager. "He's the best midfielder in the country on current form."

Certainly Currie's goalscoring form was making him a hard man to drop, and it is significant that Greenwood during this period often preferred Tony to his own erstwhile Upton Park protégé, Trevor Brooking, despite the fact that Brooking's understanding with Kevin Keegan was considered by many pundits to be England's most effective attacking weapon.

Even though a thigh injury ruled Tony out of the two European Championship qualifiers against Denmark in September and the Republic of Ireland in October (which resulted in a 4-3 win in Copenhagen and a 1-1 draw in Dublin), when the next England fixture rolled around – a Wembley date with reigning European champions Czechoslovakia on 29th November – Currie was back in the starting eleven.

Unfortunately, a frozen Wembley pitch ensured the evening was not one for the purist. Although the Czechs coped better with the icy conditions, and indeed dominated the game, they could find no way past Peter Shilton, who was in imperious form throughout.

In the 68th minute, however, the game was settled, very much against the run of play, when Nottingham Forest's right-back Viv Anderson (who created history that night by becoming the first black player to be capped by England) released Currie down the right flank. When Currie delivered a low cross into the goalmouth Pavel Michalik the Czech goalkeeper and defender Jurkemik collided with each other on the treacherous surface leaving Steve Coppell the simple task of tapping in the match-clincher.

Currie's next two games for England were both against Northern Ireland: firstly the European Championship qualifier in February (the only qualifier and therefore the only game of any competitive importance that Currie would play for Greenwood and only the second, after the Poland match of 1973, of his entire international career), and, secondly, the Home International fixture in Belfast.

Though both games resulted in straightforward England wins – 4-0 and 2-0 respectively – Tony had begun to think that playing international football was not all it was cracked up to be: "I used to come off the pitch thinking, 'Well, what was that all about?' It was great to be in the side but I always came off wondering what I'd contributed. I couldn't relax because I always felt as if I had to prove myself every time. I played five times in a row under Ramsey and that was my best run. It's not easy playing for England unless you're Butch Wilkins or Kevin Keegan and the other players play around you, and that only comes with familiarity."

Currie only experienced the pressure that came with representing his country on one more occasion – in the turgid goalless draw with Sweden on 10th June 1979 in Stockholm in which Currie was replaced by Trevor Brooking.

Although Greenwood named him in his next three England squads (against Austria, Denmark and Northern Ireland) despite the fact that an injury to his left knee had left him unfit to train let alone play in the latter two games, Tony was then jettisoned without so much as a courtesy phone call.

In the 14 games that followed his recall to the national side, Currie had been involved in ten of England's games. Interestingly, England had been unbeaten in all 14 fixtures. The game that immediately preceded Currie's recall and the one that followed his final cap were both lost!

England's 4-3 defeat to Austria turned out to be a temporary blip, however, as Greenwood's team embarked on a march of six straight wins (including an impressive 3-1 victory over world champions Argentina), securing qualification for the European Championship finals in the process. For Currie, who was now playing Second Division football following his move to QPR, another recall must have seemed remote at best. Not only would Greenwood be understandably reluctant to change a winning team, but the emergence during this run of fixtures of West Brom's Bryan Robson (who, incidentally, nominated Tony as his favourite player in a *Match Weekly* Q&A in February 1980) and Spurs play-maker Glenn Hoddle in particular, as younger and fitter midfield alternatives, probably did the most to hasten the end of Tony's international career.

A sublimely talented player very much in the Currie mould, Hoddle had made his debut in England's 2-0 win against Bulgaria in November 1979 and had played a blinder; setting up Dave Watson for the first goal with a teasing cross before adding the second himself with a half volley, side-footed into the roof of the net from just outside the Bulgarian 18-yard box. It was the sort of goal Currie himself would have been proud to score.

Despite being pushed down the pecking order, there was no reason to assume that Currie had to give up hope completely. Liverpool's David Johnson, for example, was recalled in February 1980 after an absence of five years, while West Ham's Frank Lampard Sr. and Forest's Larry Lloyd were both recalled in May 1980 after absences of eight. Nor did age seem to be a factor in Greenwood's thinking – of England's outfield players Emlyn Hughes, Trevor Brooking and Mick Mills were all older than Currie and were still getting regular games; in the case of the latter two up to and including the 1982 World Cup finals.

For Currie, though, there would be no way back and as a result it was Hoddle's name (alongside those of Brooking, Wilkins and Ray Kennedy) and not his that Greenwood included in his squad for the European Championship finals in 1980 – the first time England had qualified for the final stages of anything for ten years.

While Currie sincerely believes that he was worthy of "at least 50 caps", ultimately he would have to settle for 17. Few in number are the pundits, players and fans that believe that this total was anything but woefully scant.

"Tony was one of the best long-ball passers probably I've ever seen and he also scored a number of explosive goals," extolled Trevor Brooking, the player who arguably did more than most to restrict Tony's international appearances, certainly under Greenwood. "He got quite a number of England caps but ability wise it should have been a lot more."

While it is unlikely to represent even the smallest crumb of comfort, Currie's 17 caps *was* still significantly more and spanned more years than those other celebrated misfits of the English game with whom he is so frequently grouped: Rodney Marsh won only nine caps, Worthington eight, Bowles five, Osgood four (including two as substitute),

Hudson two and George one. Perhaps, at least in this regard, Currie was born in the wrong era. Under a coach like Sven-Goran Eriksson Currie may have won more than 17 caps, especially during an era when the nation were screaming for a player capable of filling the left side of midfield.

Additionally, with the relaxation of the laws regarding substitutions, the protection of players who play for the so-called "Big Four" clubs, and the fact that England now play more games than they did in the 1970s (due to television's demands for more friendly games, the increased number of countries allowed entry into the qualification processes for the European Championship and World Cup, and the fact that England now, as a general rule, qualify for the finals of these tournaments), Currie would surely have gotten closer to the 50 caps he so richly deserved.

While the lax substitution laws allowed Eriksson to dish caps out like confetti in friendlies, thus devaluing their currency, even this doesn't adequately explain why somehow a player as abjectly ordinary as Phil Neville, a player not fit to lace the boots of the bloke who polished Tony Currie's boots (at QPR this was future Northern Ireland international Alan McDonald), has won more England caps than all of the so-called mavericks put together!!

Most good continental sides, quite rightly, would regard this situation as risible, although, in truth, such a profoundly depressing statistic *could* only occur in England. As Rick Broadbent wrote in *The Times* in 2006: "Had Currie been born in France, the home of Michel Platini, or the Netherlands, where Dennis Bergkamp was brought up, he might have been a global star. England, though, has long dragged its heels and, in terms of football evolution, its knuckles."

When Currie finally left the England set-up, the poisoned luxury player chalice was handed to Glenn Hoddle. When Hoddle made his debut in 1979 a brilliant future seemed to beckon. While Hoddle had the talent to unlock the world's best sides, instead of being the first name on the team sheet the Tottenham playmaker spent the next nine years repeatedly sidelined by a procession of infinitely less talented but harder-working drones.

"He got 50 caps but he should have got 100," Currie suggests with characteristic generosity towards the man who effectively replaced him. "It took England two or three years before they decided he was up to it. All pro footballers could see he was the man for the job, but they'd bring him on as sub, like they did with Gascoigne to start with, and it was obvious he should have been on from the beginning. Maybe people have something against flair. It doesn't mean you're airy-fairy, though, because you can pass the ball."

In the judgement of respected football journalist Brian Glanville, "Hoddle's case was the classical one in the history of English football: the brilliant unorthodox footballer worries the mediocrities."

Glanville could so easily have been referring to Tony Currie and perhaps as long as England remain a national side prepared to hand Phil Neville in excess of 50 caps, or, for that matter Ray "the Crab" Wilkins in excess of 80, it will remain perpetual also-rans, mired in "do-I-not-like-thats," holding midfielders, broken metatarsals, defeats on penalties and the debatable merits of Steve McClaren's wisdom.

10

1979–81

"I settled very well straight away, because they were a good bunch of lads, and if the crowd take to you straight away, which they did, then that's 60 or 70 per cent of settling in. The dressing room was a great place to be."

– Tony Currie

HAVING arrived at Elland Road too late for the Revie years, Currie once again found himself joining a club on a downward curve.

For a brief period in the mid-seventies, Queens Park Rangers was London's most fashionable club. With a squad that boasted the likes of Gerry Francis, Dave Thomas, Ian Gillard, Phil Parkes, the late Dave Clement, Scottish international Don Masson, Irish international Don Givens, vastly experienced professionals like John Hollins, Ernie Howe, Frank McLintock and David Webb, as well as the extravagantly gifted Stan Bowles, QPR had enjoyed by far the most successful period in the club's history. Respected for their free-flowing football under the stewardship of

Dave Sexton, at the end of the 1975-76 season Rangers had finished runners-up in the First Division, a mere point behind champions Liverpool. The following season Sexton's men reached the quarter-final of the UEFA Cup, but following Sexton's move to Manchester United in 1977 the team started to break up and Rangers subsequently declined as a footballing force. At the end of the 1978-79 season QPR were relegated. Ironically, the game that condemned Rangers to the Second Division was the 4-3 defeat they suffered at the hands of Leeds United, in what would prove to be Tony Currie's penultimate league game for the Yorkshire club.

Relegation prompted a further exodus of players and by the time Currie arrived only left-back Ian Gillard and the talismanic Bowles remained of the team that had taken Rangers to within a nose hair of the title.

In the stead of the experienced professionals who had departed for pastures new QPR placed their faith in youth – goalkeeper Chris Woods (Docherty's £250,000 summer buy from Nottingham Forest – 19 years old at the start of the season), strikers Paul Goddard (19) and Clive Allen (18), midfielder Gary Waddock (17), defenders Steve Wicks (22), Glenn Roeder (23) and Bob Hazell (20). With the experience of Gillard, Bowles and Currie alongside these tyros, QPR looked to have enough quality to regain their seat at the top table at the first time of asking.

Certainly Currie seemed to think so: "I have tremendous respect for Tommy Docherty and I see no reason why Queens Park Rangers shouldn't go straight back to the First Division. We have some fine youngsters like Glenn Roeder, Clive Allen and Billy Hamilton, and with David McCreery and Chris Woods and Bob Hazell there besides myself we have the nucleus of a fine side.

"There are also Ian Gillard, Don Shanks, Martyn Busby, Stan Bowles and Ernie Howe, who've been here a little longer and that makes for a pretty good squad."

After failing to sign Currie for Manchester United all those years ago, Docherty was delighted to finally get his man: "I only bet on certainties and there is no gamble here," the Doc declared, despite the fact Currie portentously turned up for his medical at Loftus Road on crutches. "Our man is world class. Compare his fee with that being asked by Ray Wilkins [Butch had recently moved from Chelsea to Manchester United for £800,000]. Ray is a fabulous player, but he's a long way from being as good as Tony. It's up to me to give the punters what they want and Tony will put thousands on the gate at Loftus Road."

Characteristically, Currie was more self-deprecating about the move: "I think they were desperate. I suffered a bad ankle injury playing against PSV Eindhoven in my final game for Leeds.

"I slid into this tackle and instead of getting the ball, I hit the man's boot. It was like hitting a brick wall. I carried on for two minutes and then came off, and in the dressing room they put ice bags on it but there wasn't any bruising. It was as if everything had been stretched, even the bone itself.

"When I went to Loftus Road I was on crutches. How I passed the medical I just don't know."

In a move that would be unthinkable in the age of greedy agents and overrated full-backs almost crashing their Ferraris in disgust at offers of £55,000 a week, Currie signed a blank contract. "Jim Gregory said he'd give me £500 a week and fill in the details later," Currie explained, "so I said fair enough."

Despite dropping down a division Currie remained optimistic that it would not affect his international prospects: "Trevor Brooking and Ray Wilkins have both had to play in the Second and they managed to retain their sharpness and their England places. I think Ron Greenwood is very loyal like that. If I play well enough I'm sure he will retain me in his squad, if I don't I can't expect to be in there anyway."

Although the move had not been made for footballing reasons, playing for QPR did at least offer Currie the prospect of lining up alongside that other mercurial crowd-pleaser – Stanley Bowles. The sight of arguably the two most accomplished English showmen of their generation in tandem was, put simply, a mouth-watering prospect for the paying fans.

Bowles, too, was excited at the opportunity of teaming up with his fellow maverick, believing the signing of Currie (whose passing ability Bowles greatly admired) was precisely the shot in the arm his own career needed. "I was really looking forward to playing alongside [Tony]," Bowles revealed in his autobiography. "I thought we could build a partnership that would revitalise my game. In the past few years, I had climbed the same mountain half a dozen times with the same club; and everything was going stale. I desperately needed a new challenge, and felt that Tony could help me put the enthusiasm back into my game."

As it was, Currie's ankle injury restricted him to only two training sessions before he was finally able to make his QPR debut, in the League Cup second round second leg tie at Bradford City on 5th September.

Symbolically, Currie was handed the sacred number ten shirt previously graced by Rodney Marsh and Stan Bowles. Their displays in the shirt had bestowed upon the shirt such an iconic status that some players had previously been reluctant to wear it for fear of being compared to Marsh and Bowles. Currie had no such qualms.

"Getting the number ten shirt just seemed automatic, really," Currie later commented matter-of-factly. "There was no talking about it, I just took it over. I had the number ten shirt at Sheffield United and Leeds. It was my number, and of course number ten is *the* shirt. I mean, Pele, Maradona, innit?"

Although Bowles was hurt to have lost the right to wear the coveted number ten shirt, he generously acknowledged that Currie was a worthy successor.

"Tommy Docherty believed that the number you had on your shirt didn't matter; so I lost the right to wear the number ten shirt. He didn't realise that, at QPR, the fans expected that shirt to be worn by someone special. When he gave it to some of the other players early on in the season, they soon got rid of it. They couldn't handle the pressure of being expected to do something out of the ordinary, simply because they were wearing the shirt that Rodney and myself had made famous. Fortunately for Tommy, Tony Currie took the shirt and wore it throughout the season. I didn't mind Tony having it because he was a great player."

Despite helping his team to a 2-0 away win (to register a 4-1 aggregate win), Tony's QPR debut was not the most comfortable of occasions. Not only did he play through the pain barrier but he also had to endure an extended period of barracking from the Bradford fans, who blamed him unfairly for the injury that put their skipper Mick Bates out of the match.

In the 58th minute Bates had raced with Currie for a ball that was running out of play. While Currie had sensibly dodged out of the way, Bates, unable to stop, had crashed face first into an iron gate behind the cinder track.

Following the match, Tony's ankle injury was causing him so much pain that he was unable to train and only a series of pain-killing injections enabled him to make his home debut three days later against Rangers' West London rivals, Fulham.

For Rangers fans, however, the unveiling of their new number ten was well worth the wait. While crowds of 12,652 and 13,091 had watched the first two home games of the season against Bristol Rovers and Leicester City respectively, Currie's home debut attracted an attendance of over 17,000.

Together for the first time at Loftus Road, Currie and Bowles ran riot, inspiring Rangers to a comprehensive 3-0 victory, with the former, having been teed up by the latter, scoring the third with a stunning 30-yard volley that earned him a standing ovation.

"I remember the goal and that game," Currie later reminisced. "I scored the third in our 3-0 win. Stan Bowles dribbled down the right-hand side and the Fulham defence were pushing out to get us offside. I made a diagonal run through the middle as I always used to do in my career. Stan played a beautiful pass in over my shoulder. It dropped just nicely for me and I didn't even have to change my stride. I hit it full on the volley for a dipper.

"When it went in, the feeling was fantastic. Brilliant. I mean in your first league game for a new club it was all you could have hoped for."

"Tony Currie tormented Fulham with his control and majestic passing," genuflected Peter Gorman in the *News of the World*, "and he finally crushed them with a 73rd minute goal that earned a standing ovation. Currie has only had two training sessions with Rangers since leaving Leeds, but he was superb in his home debut for the Londoners."

Such was the manner of QPR's victory – which also marked the Loftus Road debuts of Steve Burke and Bob

Hazell – that there were some forecasting it as a turning point in the club's history; Tommy Docherty among them: "If [Tony's] like that on one leg, what'll he be like with two?

"I can visualise Currie and Bowles forming a devastating partnership in the Second Division," Docherty continued. "Bowles needs a class player around him and he certainly has one now."

On the whole, Currie was pleased with his Loftus Road debut. "I caught one ball wrong that I volleyed in the first half, but apart from that things went all right," Currie remarked at full-time. "Mind you, I could have done with another injection at half-time, but then the goal came and that was that.

"As for playing in the same side as Stan, well Stan is a really good player. He is what I call telepathic. I can tell more or less where he is going to stick the ball. I think we're going to get on great on the pitch."

Although injuries restricted Currie's appearances in the first half of the 1978-79 season, when he and Bowles *were* able to take to the field together QPR's midfield proved irresistible. While Currie and Bowles were given licence to express themselves, Tommy Docherty shrewdly detailed the combative David McCreery to play the holding role and do the donkey work to which the two former England internationals were temperamentally unsuited. "Tony Currie and myself were both creative players," Bowles explains, "and Dave McCreery, an Irish lad who had played for Manchester United under Docherty, was the terrier so it was a good blend. McCreery's job was to win the ball and give it to me, or Tony, to create openings.

"I started the season playing in midfield," Bowles continues, "but more in the middle of the park because Tony was a right-sided player. We immediately fitted into midfield very well together, and I started to enjoy playing with him."

Although Currie and Bowles only played seven league games together, they were never on the losing side. Indeed, when Currie made his debut on 8th September Rangers were sitting in 20th place. Thirteen games later, the form of Currie and Bowles and the prolific goalscoring pairing of Clive Allen and Paul Goddard had taken Rangers to top of the league.

Rangers' spell at the top of the table, however, was all too brief. A defeat away at Cambridge (in Currie's absence) and a 2-2 draw at home to Wrexham (in which Currie was used as a substitute) knocked Rangers off their perch.

The Wrexham game was also significant for being Stan Bowles' last game in a Queens Park Rangers shirt. With Rangers lying in fifth place, Bowles (who, it is said, did not get on with Tommy Docherty) was transferred to the reigning champions of Europe, Nottingham Forest, for £250,000.

While Tommy Docherty was of the view that the transfer was "a good deal for Rangers, a good deal for Forest, but most of all a good deal for Stan", the sale of Bowles ultimately proved to be a shattering blow to Rangers' promotion aspirations.

From a footballing perspective, Currie was as disappointed as anyone: "It was a joy to briefly play with him because he was on the same wavelength as me... He was still the star. The fans loved him because he was still there even when all the 1976 side had split up. I certainly didn't take any star rating off him. We all knew he'd be leaving and it was a shame."

Despite the form of Goddard and Allen (a partnership which ended the season with 44 league goals), and the quality of the team's football in general, Docherty's young and inexperienced side struggled to keep up with the promotion-chasing pack and a seven-game winless run between December and January, in addition to a ten-match run between March and April that included seven draws, saw all promotion hopes disappear. The club ended the season in fifth place, four points adrift of promotion.

It was very much a case of what might have been. If injury had not restricted Currie to 27 starts (plus one appearances as sub), and if Bowles had not been sold at such a critical stage of the season, the team would surely have been able to turn enough of those costly draws into wins.

* * * * *

Nevertheless Currie became a very popular player among the fans and in the dressing room, too. Centre-half and club captain Glenn Roeder regarded Currie as a "flawed genius". "He could play off both feet," Roeder opined. "He weighed about 14 stone and he had no pace but he could surge with that ball, across the halfway line and deep into enemy territory. I don't think Tony would mind me saying he had a few personal problems, though."

Currie's personal problems were still primarily domestic in nature. The move to London, it seemed, had done nothing to improve his marital relationship. "Within a year of moving back we were divorced. She probably felt her depression was down to me."

Back at Loftus Road, there were strong rumours that his failure to lead Rangers back to the top flight was about to cost Tommy Docherty his job. As he had done at Leeds, Currie led a deputation to chairman Jim Gregory's office to save the manager's job. "Tommy Docherty was about to get the sack," Currie recalls, "so six of us went to see Jim Gregory and we saved his job for about a month, too."

It proved only a temporary respite. Whatever hopes Docherty had of keeping his job were dealt a fatal blow when the prolific strike pairing of Clive Allen and Paul Goddard were both sold. In June Clive Allen became the first million-pound teenager when he was sold for £1.2 million to Arsenal (who then let him go to Crystal Palace without allowing him a single first team appearance) while Paul Goddard was offloaded to West Ham United for £750,000.

Unfortunately the money was not re-invested in the team but went towards the modernisation of Loftus Road. With Rangers forced to sell their best players to help finance their ground, Currie must have thought it was like the early 1970s at Bramall Lane all over again!

Although Docherty and chairman Jim Gregory were heavily criticised for offloading three strikers (having also sold Mickey Walsh to Porto for £170,000), Docherty was unrepentant: "It was terrific business for the club. We paid £750,000 for a new stand at one end of the ground making it seating around three-quarters of the ground. We paid that off and had £1.25 million left through the sale of the two players. In my book, that's terrific business and good news for the future of QPR Football Club. People say we've weakened the team. I disagree. Selling Allen and Goddard has done nothing to our chances of promotion. We are a stronger side all round and are creating chances. Tony Currie has solved his domestic problems and has started well, and we have Tommy Langley, young but experienced, from Chelsea. Why are we weak?"

In Rangers' first home game of the 1980-81 season, against Bristol Rovers, Docherty pitched unknown 17-year-old Wayne Fereday into the attack and appeared to have been vindicated when the teenage debutant scored twice in the 4-0 win.

Unfortunately the win against Bristol Rovers proved to be QPR's only success (and Fereday's only goals of the season) during a disastrous start to the campaign. After only one win from the first seven games, Docherty had to go and in October 1980, he was sacked as Queens Park Rangers' manager.

To take over the reins, Rangers turned to Crystal Palace boss and former Hoop Terry Venables. With Rangers hovering near the foot of the table, Venables quickly set about strengthening the squad, bringing in Currie's former Sheffield United team-mate Simon Stainrod, a £275,000 capture from Oldham Athletic.

Having sold Chris Woods to First Division Norwich City for £225,000 in December to finance further purchases, Venables then went back to cash-strapped Crystal Palace and, over the course of the season, scooped up half their first team – bringing in John Burridge, Mike Flanagan, Terry Fenwick, Gerry Francis and Tony Sealy. Having also taken his entire Palace backroom staff (assistant manager Allan Harris, youth team coach George Graham, chief scout Arnie Warren and physiotherapist Dave Butler) with him to Loftus Road, Venables' raid on Selhurst Park was controversial to say the least.

"Palace complained I was taking unfair advantage of them," Venables recalls in his autobiography, "but the players could see the club's parlous financial state as well as I could, and shared my view that QPR were going places, while Palace were going nowhere fast…Simon Stainrod also arrived as I tried to strengthen areas of the team that looked weak around players whom I thought were good enough."

One player that Venables definitely did think was good enough was Tony Currie, who the new manager rated as highly as that other Loftus Road idol, Rodney Marsh. "Currie had the same skills as Rodney, but was a very different player," Venables stated. "He was very strong and much tougher than Rodney. Tony played slightly further back than Rodney and took a more responsible role, and if Marsh scored more goals, Currie had more of an all-round game. He had any amount of individual ability, but he was a team player and popular with his team-mates, and like Stan Bowles, should certainly have played for England much more often than he did."

Venables' arrival gave everyone at the club a tremendous boost, lifting the gloom that had begun to settle like a pall under Docherty, and the players were particularly stimulated by his refreshing coaching methods and ideas. Whereas Docherty had reportedly encouraged his players to play off the cuff, Venables brought organisation back to Loftus Road and it showed in the results.

Indeed, there were many who believed that QPR's chances of promotion would have been greatly enhanced if Terry Venables had arrived at Loftus Road a month earlier than he did.

As it was the indifferent start to the season and the upheavals caused by Docherty's departure, allied to the sale and initial failure to adequately replace Clive Allen and Paul Goddard, ultimately scuppered Rangers' chances of returning to the First Division. In light of these factors it was hardly surprising that QPR were never seriously in contention for promotion throughout the 1980-81 season. Disappointingly, Rangers finished the season in eighth place, 23 points behind champions West Ham.

Although injury restricted Currie to 31 League appearances (his best total during his four seasons at Loftus Road), Tony was convinced 1980-81 represented his best season ever in terms of personal form, and his fellow professionals evidently agreed – voting him into the PFA Second Division "Team of the Year".

"It's certainly as good as the three best seasons I had with Leeds," Currie told *Shoot!* "That may sound strange considering all the changes within the team. But a player knows when he's playing well, and when the season ended I knew I had every right to be delighted with my form. I'm 31 and I've finished my second season in Division Two. You don't get any younger and I desperately wanted to get to the First Division with Rangers at the end of [the 1980-81] season. But it wasn't to be and now we have to make sure we make it next season."

Tony was particularly excited by the prospect of developing his midfield partnership with Gerry Francis who had returned to Loftus Road in February: "It's great to have two players in the team capable of making the play," Currie remarked. "Normally, you only get one and sometimes that places too much of a burden on that player. I enjoy working with Gerry because he plays and looks upon the game in a similar way to myself. The understanding we started to create at the end of the season could really be something next season."

Currie was also impressed by the improvements Terry Venables had brought to the club in such a relatively short space of time and was supremely confident that he was the man to lead the club back to the big time. "He's approached his work with the right attitude and done it well," Currie praised. "There was a lot of work to be done, but the side has been made a hell of a lot better. We should be ready to have a crack at the promotion race next season."

11

1981–82

*"It's quite a hard surface and I should imagine
that in match conditions it will be hard on
the ankles when twisting and turning."*
— Tony Currie

DESPITE QPR's under-achievement of the
previous season, there was every reason to believe
the 1981-82 campaign would be one to remember
for success-starved Rangers supporters.

Certainly Currie had faith in his manager, ultimately
regarding Venables as the best coach he was ever privileged
to work with: "He was so positive and confident in what
he was saying. He *knew* he was right. He put everything
across so easily and didn't blind you with bloody science.
He was very astute. You could see his mind ticking over
with ideas all the time."

In the pre-season Venables had once again spent wisely
in the transfer market – bringing in the combative and
versatile John Gregory from Brighton and luring Clive
Allen back from his bizarre sojourn with Arsenal and

Crystal Palace in an exchange deal involving defender Steve Wicks.

While Venables had assembled a squad that was widely regarded as the most talented in Division Two, the most significant development at Loftus Road was the pre-season installation of an all-weather artificial playing surface (the first of its kind in the Football League). Loftus Road had long been plagued by a grass pitch that regularly turned into a mid-winter mud bath. The artificial turf was therefore seen as the best solution to the problem. Most visiting teams' unfamiliarity with the plastic turf would also serve to make Loftus Road virtually impregnable. It was therefore no surprise when QPR were made favourites to go up with the bookmakers.

Despite the prevailing perception that the £350,000 Omniturf surface would benefit the ball players of Currie's ilk, Tony had his reservations about the experiment. "People are saying that the skilful players will come into their own on this pitch, but I'm not so sure," Tony reflected after his first 90-minute practice session on the new surface, which he correctly predicted would be hard on the leg joints when twisting and turning. "The surface is so smooth and fast that the less skilful players are going to find it easier to control and pass the ball. There's no mud or uneven bounces to worry about and so the skilful players, who can operate in any conditions, won't get any real advantage. Visiting teams should soon adapt to the conditions and may even play better because of the quality surface. So I don't think there will be any real advantage to Rangers."

On the contrary; of the twenty games played at Loftus Road throughout the season, Rangers would record twenty wins, five draws and only two defeats in all competitions – one of which would come in the first home game of the season against Luton Town (who evidently enjoyed their 2-1 win so much that they later became the second side to install an artificial pitch).

While injury had kept Tony out of the Luton game he returned the following week for the resounding 3-0 win against Newcastle.

The following week Rangers succumbed to a 2-1 defeat away at Grimsby Town; a game that was also significant for marking the last time Tony would play alongside Gerry Francis, who injured himself when he crashed into a goal post against Rotherham in November (a game that Tony missed) and was unable to win back his place when he regained fitness.

Although the Hoops bounced back to beat Palace 1-0 at home two defeats were then suffered in quick succession away from home (against Oldham Athletic and Derby County), before Rangers bounced back with two 2-0 home wins against Blackburn and Norwich, with a 5-0 League Cup win against Portsmouth sandwiched in between.

The Norwich game, however, would prove to be Currie's last for over 14 weeks. With the unyielding plastic pitch having exacerbated the problems with his left knee, Currie was taken to Charing Cross Hospital for the removal of a piece of bone. It was, he admitted, an injury that had been troubling him for two months.

With Currie in fine form leading up to the injury it was a blow for both player and club. As consolation Currie received get-well cards by the sackful as well as regular visits from his large family and even larger cadre of fans.

Although the surgery was deemed successful, when the pesky bone fragment was removed from his knee and placed beside his bed as a memento it later inexplicably disappeared. Although the item would now presumably fetch a bundle on ebay as a ghoulish piece of sporting memorabilia, there was no foul play afoot. "To tell you the truth," Tony mused, "I think a cleaning lady threw it away. Yes, I would have liked to keep it."

The day after the operation Tony was up and about, albeit on crutches, and what would prove a long fight for fitness began, a fight that would be lengthened by the fact that Currie had also put on seven pounds in weight during his enforced lay-off. "That was because my mum sent me in Red Cross parcels," Currie elaborated, "with things like chicken legs, crackers, crisps. Otherwise I think I would have lost weight.

"I left hospital after two weeks," Currie recalled, "but then I had to go back every day for physiotherapy. I had to have electric treatment on the wound itself to remove the swelling, and I did weights to get the muscle back on my thigh. It had never been the same really since I had a cartilage operation eight years ago. I suppose I lost about an inch around the leg. Then I started training again."

Any thoughts of a quick return to action were put on hold when bad weather further hindered his recovery process.

"The bad weather cost me a month," Currie states. "I was meant to train at Greenford on soft ground. The surgeon said I was not to try that left leg on hard ground, or any road running."

When Currie returned to first team action after an absence of 11 league games, his fitness was tested to the limit with five games in two weeks.

Although his first game back, against Wrexham on 16th January, which marked the occasion of Tony's 500th professional league game, ended in a 1-1 draw, Currie showed that he had lost none of his ability to leave the crowd gasping at his genius.

With two minutes remaining on the clock, Currie waltzed past several defenders before hitting a shot with the outside of the foot that curled beyond the keeper's reach but agonisingly just beyond the far post.

Two days later, QPR and Currie were in action again in the twice-postponed FA Cup third round replay against Middlesbrough at Ayresome Park.

After 40 minutes Rangers led 2-0 thanks to two Simon Stainrod goals, but 'Boro pegged the score back to 2-2 and the force appeared to be with the home side as the game went into extra-time, especially when Currie went off injured. As it was, Currie's replacement, 19-year old full-back Warren Neill, snatched the dramatic extra-time winner that took Rangers into the fourth round – a result to rub in the face of the FA apparatchiks who had issued a mid-season threat to ban Rangers from the FA Cup because it was their view that the artificial Loftus Road turf afforded them an unfair advantage.

Fortunately, Tony's injury was not serious and five days later he was back in the side for the FA Cup fourth round tie against Fourth Division Blackpool at Bloomfield Road.

What should have been a stroll against lower league opposition almost turned into a proverbial banana skin. Although QPR dominated the first half, they could not translate their superiority into goals. The second half, however, was a different story as Blackpool at last sprung to life, laying siege to the Rangers goal as the visitors' attacking threat wilted. Fortunately, a stoic rearguard action led by Glenn Roeder and goalkeeper Peter Hucker, inept Blackpool finishing and one controversial refereeing decision combined to secure Rangers a replay.

The pivotal moment came on 55 minutes, when Ernie Howe flattened Blackpool's Ronnie Blair in the box. It looked a stonewall penalty.

"Ronnie was sent flying by three men," Blackpool's winger Colin Morris protested. "I have seen spot-kicks given for a lot less." Fortuitously for Rangers, referee Keith Hackett waved away Blackpool's appeals and Venables' side lived to fight another day on their own artificial turf.

Sure enough, three days later normal service was resumed at Loftus Road, with Rangers handing the Tangerines a 5-1 thrashing, with Clive Allen grabbing four of the goals.

Intriguingly, in attendance that night was one Ron Greenwood! With the 1982 World Cup only a few months away, was Currie still in his plans?

Asked if he still dreamt of a place in the World Cup squad, Currie was not only realistic about his chances but also generously urged Greenwood to keep faith with the man who had taken his place in the England set-up: "Of course I'd love to [be involved] but he has to keep faith with the players he has got and find younger players. Then I look at a player like Glenn Hoddle, who is going through just what I went through. I played for England over a period of seven years, 17 games in all. I was in and out. I never had a real run. And it's the same with him. He is a supremely talented player. I just hope he can get in, and stay in the squad."

Although Tony admitted to feeling the strain after three matches in eight days, it was not long before he was back to his best, and he was especially pleased with his contribution to QPR's 1-0 win against Grimsby Town.

"I felt really right during the game," he told Rangers' matchday programme columnist, Michael Wale. "No, I didn't feel worried when I first came back. I'd had such a lay-off and trained so much. But there is nothing like match practice. Now with all those games I'm really right."

A week later Grimsby once again provided the opposition – this time in the fifth round of the FA Cup. Although Currie was once again absent, goals from Clive Allen, Simon Stainrod and Ernie Howe gave the Hoops a 3-1 win, securing their passage into the sixth round of the cup for only the fourth time in the club's history.

Despite progress in the cup and the return of Currie, QPR still seemed incapable of delivering the goods away from home – winning only one and losing six of their next eight league games on the road.

Rangers' solitary away win during this period came on 27th February at Carrow Road, and was inspired by a vintage Currie display. "Tony Currie put on a one-man show for Rangers," wrote Pat Collins in *The Sunday People*, "and won it with a flash of genius. As Currie prepared to take a right wing corner, manager Terry Venables waved up to defender Roeder for support. Currie saw Roeder advance and picked him out perfectly with his waist-high corner.

"A great first half from both sides became a hectic scramble after the break. Norwich threw in everything… [but] all the time Currie was falling back with superb judgement to nip into home attacks and rob them of their sting."

With away wins proving elusive, Rangers' promotion hopes were being kept alive by their home form alone. Indeed, following Currie's comeback against Wrexham on 16th January, Rangers would not drop another point at home until the goalless draw with high-flying Watford on 12th April and would not concede another goal at Loftus Road in the league until the 2-1 win against Shrewsbury on 17th April. All hopes of progressing in the FA Cup, therefore, seemed to hinge on avoiding an away draw.

With Arsenal and Manchester United bowing out of the cup in the third round and Liverpool departing at the fifth round stage the competition was wide open. In fact, only three First Division teams were left in the draw at the sixth round stage – West Brom, Coventry and holders and favourites Spurs. The rest of the draw consisted of five Second Division clubs.

Fortunately for Rangers the sixth round draw was a kindly one – sparing them a tricky tie against any of the remaining First Division sides and pairing them with Crystal Palace. Propitiously, the game would be played at Loftus Road.

When the match was played on 6th March, however, it was tougher than Rangers had every right to expect, with Barron, Palace's goalkeeper, in particularly inspired form. Fortunately, a Clive Allen goal three minutes from time against his old club sent Rangers into the last four of the competition for the first time in the club's history. In an auspicious echo of their only previous appearance at Wembley (in the 1967 League Cup Final), QPR's opponents in the semi would be West Bromwich Albion.

With all thoughts turned towards the semi-final on 6th April, QPR promptly lost three of their next four league matches, which included a humiliating 4-0 thrashing at the hands of promotion rivals Watford.

After the Watford result, Venables decided to shore up the defence with yet another raid on Crystal Palace's playing staff, poaching Steve Wicks (who had left Rangers in the pre-season claiming he didn't think the new Omniturf would suit his game) one minute before the transfer window closed on 25th March for £275,000.

Wicks could barely conceal his delight at re-joining his old mates and was convinced Rangers were heading for promotion. "We've got so many players who can just

turn a match like Simon, Clive and Tony Currie," Wicks
told Michael Wale. "TC is a great friend of mine and we
always kept in touch after I had left. In fact when I signed
for Rangers, Simon and TC were the first to ring and
congratulate me. That gave me a great feeling."

Wicks made his debut on 27th March in yet another
away defeat, this time an ill-tempered 1-0 reverse at
Rotherham (which Currie missed); a game that saw three
red cards, five bookings and was marred further when
Peter Hucker was stretchered off with a jaw injury.

Fortunately a comprehensive midweek victory against
Sheffield Wednesday put them back on the winning track
and set them up nicely for their date with destiny the
following Saturday.

Their semi-final opponents, although a First Division
side, would only finish ten places above them in the
Football League pyramid and were therefore not to be
feared. However, with a side boasting the likes of Derek
Statham, Brendon Batson, John Wile, Currie's old nemesis
Ally Robertson and Cyrille Regis, one of the most powerful
and imposing centre-forwards of his day, the Baggies,
League Cup semi-finalists earlier in the year, were not to
be taken lightly, either.

The game, when it was played on that sunlit April
Saturday at Arsenal's Highbury ground, was not by any
means a classic. With Bob Hazell almost completely
nullifying the threat of Regis at one end and with Rangers
struggling to carve out any significant openings for
themselves at the other, the game appeared to be drifting
towards stalemate.

As far as Tony Currie was concerned there was good
reason for that. "Like all semi-finals," he later expounded,
"there is so much to gain by winning and so much to lose
by being beaten that the game is always tense with the

players scared to make a mistake. And both sides had the added disadvantage of playing on a Highbury pitch that wasn't very helpful to good football. It was very hard and the bounce was awkward and it made it very hard for us to play properly."

What the game desperately needed was a goal and, to the delight of the Rangers supporters, it came in the 72nd minute. Following a flowing move down Rangers' right flank, the ball was nudged into the Baggies' penalty area, where West Brom's Ally Robertson, reaching it first, looked certain to boot it into touch. Instead when the lurking Clive Allen instinctively stuck out his right leg, the ball ricocheted off the Rangers forward beyond the reach of Brom's keeper Mark Grew and into the net. What looked like a fluke was, in reality, a superb poacher's goal, capping a fairy-tale return to Highbury for the young striker.

Despite two reckless back passes in the final 17 minutes Rangers managed to cling on to their advantage to reach the FA Cup Final for the first and, to date, only time in their history. Their opponents would be holders and London rivals Tottenham Hotspur who had seen off Leicester City 2-0 in the other semi.

Most observers agreed that Currie had been instrumental in the win. "Albion had no one with the authority of Currie in midfield," praised *The Sunday Mirror*, a judgement echoed by his manager, Terry Venables: "We were the better side. We clamped down well on Cyrille Regis and big Bob Hazell did a cracking job. Tony Currie and Glenn Roeder were also outstanding. They started everything for us and, in the end I felt we were well worth our win."

After three semi-final defeats whilst a Leeds United player, Currie's satisfaction at reaching a major final for the first time in his career was understandably unconfined.

"The smile on Tony Currie's face after the semi-final triumph told a story that a thousand words could not have captured," reported the *Official QPR Souvenir Brochure*. "For Tony had finally made it to Wembley for an FA Cup final and as he signed autographs and chatted and waved to the fans before boarding the coach to leave Highbury for more celebrations he was visibly overcome with emotion."

"Getting to the cup final in 1982 was one of the highlights of my career," Tony confirmed. "It was always my ambition to play in a cup final but after going out in three semis when I was at Leeds I thought I'd never make it. I can't describe the elation I felt after we'd beaten West Brom at Highbury. It was incredible to think the dream was going to come true."

The celebrations were understandably raucous. Back at Shepherd's Bush young lads ran up and down the Uxbridge Road proudly waving their blue and white flags and if ever there was a picture of how times have changed in football, the Rangers players mingled and celebrated freely with supporters and well-wishers such as Rangers old boy Stan Bowles at the Crown and Sceptre pub. Currie and Ian Gillard even served drinks from behind the bar.

Although most clubs in Rangers' position tend to lose focus in the league once a cup final berth has been secured, Rangers knew that promotion remained easily within their grasp. After a 3-0 win at home to Orient on 6th April, Rangers lay in seventh place – only three points behind third placed Sheffield Wednesday over whom they had a game in hand.

With a date at Wembley secured, Currie was revelling in another purple period of form, rolling back the years to turn in a vintage performance.

"Tony Currie fired Spurs a Wembley warning as QPR surged back into the Second Division promotion race last night," wrote *The Sun*'s Alasdair Ross. "Currie turned on a masterful display to set up a strolling victory that blasted Rangers into the heart of the traffic jam of clubs at the top."

Unfortunately, the cup run and the fixture congestion that had inevitably accompanied it meant very few Rangers fans were there that night to see it.

"Last night's crowd of 10,531 was Rangers' sixth lowest gate of the season," Ross continued, "nearly 3,000 down on their average attendance – and it must have been a bitter disappointment so soon after their semi-final triumph over West Brom. But the fans who did show up were treated to a magnificent performance from former England midfield man Currie. He was at his supreme best and it was no surprise when he set up the first goal in the 28th minute. Currie drilled a free kick to the near post, centre-half Bob Hazell cleverly back headed the ball on and Orient goalkeeper Mervyn Day could only help it home."

After a frustrating defeat at Chelsea's Stamford Bridge four days later – a game Rangers had dominated with their crisp passing and intelligent running off the ball – Rangers returned to winning ways at Loftus Road a week later against Shrewsbury.

However, the 2-1 victory against the Shrews was marred by the sight of Currie limping off five minutes from time with an ankle injury – an injury which side-lined Tony for Rangers' next five games and also put Tony's participation in the FA Cup Final in serious doubt.

"It's the ankle injury he's had for about three weeks," Venables ominously told *The News of the World*.

For Venables and Queens Park Rangers it was a real body blow. "Over the past few weeks he has been playing as well as he has ever done," Venables stated, "and during that time he has looked as good as any player in the country."

Currie's latest injury setback couldn't have come at a worse time for QPR whose cup heroics had led to a fixture backlog that meant they had to play their last five games in 15 days.

Although impressive away wins against Cardiff (which inched them to within two points of third placed Sheffield Wednesday with a game in hand) and Newcastle, which sandwiched a handsome 7-1 demolition of Bolton Wanderers at Loftus Road, suggested all thoughts of the Twin Towers had been banished from the dressing room, the woeful away form that had dogged them all season returned to bite them with two consecutive defeats against Barnsley and then champions-elect Luton. With Norwich City mounting a late surge, these two defeats effectively ended QPR's interest in the promotion race.

Although Currie did return for the final league game of the season – a 2-1 win against Cambridge United – to prove his fitness for Wembley, by then none of the three promoted teams – Luton, Watford and Norwich – could be caught and QPR ended the season in fifth place, a mere two points away from a return to the top flight.

It had been a Jekyll and Hyde season for QPR. Although 15 league games had been won at Loftus Road, 13 were lost away and that's where promotion had ultimately been lost.

12

Cup Final

"Win or lose we'll have some booze"
– Terry Venables, speaking
before the 1982 FA Cup Final

THE 1982 FA Cup Final took place on 22nd May 1982 at Wembley Stadium. QPR's opponents, Tottenham Hotspur, were the holders of the trophy, and were hot favourites to retain it.

Tottenham had never lost a cup final in six attempts and could boast a team of stars, among them the potent strike partnership of Garth Crooks and Scottish international Steve Archibald, plus household names like Ray Clemence and Currie's successor to the crown of England's most misunderstood midfield playmaker, Glenn Hoddle.

Furthermore the Tottenham side contained eight players who had played every minute of their two games against Manchester City in the 1981 final (Archibald, Galvin, Hoddle, Crooks, Hughton, Miller, Roberts and Perryman), while goalkeeper Clemence had also played in three FA Cup finals – once as a winner in 1974 – with

Liverpool. That made nine players with FA Cup final winning experience.

In addition, Tottenham were making their fifth Wembley appearance in a little over a year, following the 1981 FA Cup Final and its replay, the Charity Shield and the 1982 League Cup Final, in which they had been beaten by Liverpool.

The QPR team, meanwhile, could boast no such experience. Indeed, only Currie and Gillard had played in big Wembley occasions, having played there ten times and two times respectively for England.

As a result, Rangers' management and players were all looking to Currie to inspire the team to cup final victory. "Tony should enjoy himself at Wembley," Glenn Roeder confidently predicted. "He'll love the open spaces and being up against a side like Spurs who will let him play a bit."

"There has been some silly talk about how we are just making up the numbers at Wembley," Terry Venables scoffed prior to the match. "How can people say that when we have players in our team like Tony Currie? Imagine Tony at Wembley. He's never been there before [*sic*], it may be his last chance and he'll have the perfect stage to prove what a good player he is."

Predictably much of the pre-match hype focused on the showdown between Currie and Tottenham's equally gifted maestro Glenn Hoddle, almost certainly England's finest ball-players of the 1970s and 1980s respectively. It was a battle of wits that Hoddle claimed to be looking forward to with relish: "We're great friends, similar in style, and our battle should prove an interesting side issue," the Spurs man told *Shoot!* "If Tony plays well, Rangers will be dangerous. He is one of their best players, a man for the big occasion. His passing is immaculate, and although

I have never copied another player's style, I must confess his long-range passing and sharp eye for a weakness in a defence has influenced my game. We'll have to watch him particularly closely in free-kick situations… Tony will try to seize this opportunity to put on a show, to climax his career."

Tony, meanwhile, was planning to make the most of his first cup final. "I plan to savour as much of the atmosphere as I can," he promised. "Since the semi-final I have been enjoying every minute of the feeling of getting to Wembley and I couldn't have had a better boost at this stage in my career."

Strangely, Currie would take his place in QPR's cup final line-up wearing the unfamiliar number seven jersey, Venables having handed Tony's favoured number ten shirt to Simon Stainrod.

In the event the 1982 FA Cup Final was a cagey non-event, with few clear-cut chances. Although Peter Hucker was the busier keeper (earning him the Man of the Match award), Spurs were largely restricted to unthreatening long-range pot shots.

QPR's own attacking options, meanwhile, were dealt a shattering blow when Clive Allen was crocked early in the game and was effectively a spectator until he eventually limped off five minutes into the second half, whereupon he was replaced by Gary Micklewhite.

A goalless 90 minutes pushed the game into extra-time where the deadlock was finally broken on 110 minutes when a shot from Glenn Hoddle (which took a miniscule deflection off Currie's calf) found the right-hand corner of Hucker's goal.

Rangers, though, refused to lie down. With only five minutes left on the clock, Simon Stainrod took a long throw about ten yards from the Spurs goal line that was flicked on at the near post by Bob Hazell, where Terry Fenwick was on hand to nod the ball past Spurs keeper Ray Clemence for a deserved Rangers equaliser, taking the FA Cup Final to a replay for a second year running.

When the replay was staged five days later, Tottenham were able to field the same eleven that had started on Saturday, while Rangers were two key men down. Clive Allen had not recovered from his injury while Glenn Roeder was farcically suspended thanks to a booking picked up some weeks earlier.

Despite such setbacks, the first match had shown that QPR and Spurs were actually two fairly evenly matched sides, and Rangers, skippered by Currie in Roeder's absence, had every reason to approach the replay with a renewed sense of confidence.

"Spurs did very well in the first game," Currie observed, "but we kept in it and took them to a replay. I captained the side because Glenn Roeder was suspended. I was thinking, 'This is it. This is my dream to be in a cup final at Wembley and winning the cup.' Being captain as well, I thought it was all set for me to lift the cup."

After only six minutes of the replay, Currie's premonition appeared to be in tatters, when Tottenham's Graham Roberts aggressively burst through Rangers' vacant midfield and into the penalty area. With no one else seemingly prepared to make a challenge of significance, Currie made a desperate lunge to win the ball but only succeeded in bringing Roberts down. It was a clear penalty.

"Graham Roberts picked the ball up in the midfield and ran at our defence," Currie recalls. "At one point he overran the ball and Bob Hazell had a chance to move in and take it off him but for some reason he sat back. I'd been tracking Graham all the way and when he got into the box I dived in with a sliding tackle just as he pulled his foot back. I caught his foot so it was a penalty, yes, but I was going for the ball. If I'd have done it today they would have given me the bloody guillotine. You only have to breathe on someone now and it's a penalty."

From the resulting penalty Glenn Hoddle made no mistake, nonchalantly sending Peter Hucker the wrong way to give his side the lead.

Immediately prior to the interval, Rangers seemed to have equalised. A free kick was chipped into a crowded Spurs penalty area where the ball eventually broke to the lively Gary Micklewhite who rifled a superb finish past Clemence from the edge of the area. However, the goal was harshly ruled out by referee Clive White because Terry Fenwick had strayed marginally offside when the original ball into the box had been played. To add salt to the injustice under today's rules the goal would almost certainly have been allowed to stand.

Rangers left the field a goal down, and a strangely quiet Currie, looking only half-fit, trudged off to face the music.

"I got a right roasting from Terry Venables at half-time," Currie recalls. "'You shouldn't have dived in because Peter Hucker would have saved it,' he said."

Inspired by Venables' half-time team-talk, it was a different Currie who emerged for the second half, contributing manfully as QPR did their best to force an equaliser. In fact, Currie was at the heart of everything as a spirited Rangers side pushed Spurs squarely on to the back foot.

Although Rangers were the side likeliest to score in the second half, testing the Spurs defence to the limit and forcing Ray Clemence into action several times, the closest Rangers came was when John Gregory's volleyed cross-shot agonisingly hit the crossbar.

Instead, Glenn Hoddle's sixth-minute penalty remained the only goal of the replay and after three and a half hours of football, Spurs had retained the trophy.

For Currie being in a final had failed to live up to his expectations: "Being there was wonderful but the event itself was a disappointment. Good side though they were, we could have beaten Tottenham, who had had a very tough season, but Mike Flanagan and Simon Stainrod had stinkers in both games. Simon thought he could beat them on his own but nine times out of ten he would run at the defence and lose the ball."

Despite the defeat when Tony went up to collect his medal it was the partial realisation of a childhood dream: "I always said in the old *Shoot!* magazines when they asked, 'What would you like to do more than anything?' And I always said, 'To play in the cup final in front of the Queen and go up and get my medal off the Queen.' In the end it was Princess Anne, so I nearly got there.

"We were really unlucky not to beat Tottenham that night. I gave away the penalty early on from which Glenn Hoddle scored. But we dictated the rest of the game. John Gregory hit the bar with a terrific lob and Gary Micklewhite had a perfectly good goal disallowed. So our 1-0 defeat was a real shame."

Tony knew that his last chance to win a major trophy had passed him by. "I was suffering injury problems by then," Currie explained. "I'd had a cartilage out when I was 24 and by the time I was 29 or 30, the knee was starting to give me a few problems. [The] Astroturf pitch down at Loftus Road...didn't do me any favours at all. It probably cut my career by about three or four years."

While Hoddle took his place in England's World Cup squad that summer (where he was used sparingly), Currie watched his country fritter away a perfectly good chance to win the 1982 World Cup in Spain from his sofa. Although England returned unbeaten from their five games and conceded only one goal, Ron Greenwood's men crucially failed to create enough chances (and failed to convert those that they did) in their second round group game encounters against West Germany and the host nation and flew home early.

Might things have been different if Greenwood had kept faith with Currie? At 32 years of age it certainly hadn't been too late for Tony. Certainly with 33-year-olds Trevor Brooking and Mick Mills in the squad and very much part of Greenwood's preferred starting eleven, age would not have been a bar. Perhaps Currie could have even been an asset as an impact player, especially when they desperately needed a break in the dying throes against Spain.

Regrettably, we shall never know.

13

1983–Present

*"It would be beyond the belief of modern-
day players with an iota of his talent that,
at the age of 33, a star such as Currie was
living with his mother in a council house and
downing four bottles of whisky a week."*
— Rick Broadbent writing in
The Times, 2006

THANKS to a knee ligament tear sustained in a
friendly four days before the season began, Tony
missed the start of the 1982-83 campaign. However,
although the left knee continued to give him trouble
throughout August and September, by October Currie
was deemed fit enough to turn out for the Rangers reserve
side.

After a run of four games in the Football Combination
Tony was able to force his way back into first team
consideration, coming on as a second half substitute in
the 2-0 win against Bolton on 30th October. At first it
seemed as though it was business as usual.

"Tony Currie, playing his first match since the FA Cup Final replay, made an impressive return as Queens Park Rangers moved to second place in Division Two after this win," wrote John Etheridge in *The Sunday Express*. "He came on as a substitute after 61 minutes and quickly showed many of the neat touches that made him an England international during the '70s. Rangers' manager Terry Venables said, 'Tony's suffered no reaction. He is a quality player and I was pleased with the way he fitted in again.'"

Venables was so pleased that, a fortnight later, he handed Currie a starting berth for the visit to Loftus Road of Blackburn Rovers. By his own admission Tony had a stinker in the 2-2 draw and never played for the Rangers first XI again. Currie later admitted that he shouldn't have played in the Blackburn game due to his injury: "Looking back it was an absolute nightmare. I was just not fit enough and I let myself and the side down. I was sick because I had been dying to get back in the side. I knew it was a great opportunity for me to reclaim my place but it turned out to be probably the worst game of my career."

Venables evidently agreed and demoted Currie to the reserve team for whom he was virtually ever present until ligament trouble returned in the second half of January.

Although Currie did appreciate that Venables would be wrong to change a winning team he made no secret of the fact that he was deeply unhappy playing in the reserves: "I appreciate that the manager has a winning side at the moment and it would be wrong for him to change it just for me. I'm really down in the dumps because I miss the excitement and build-up to a Saturday match and I miss playing in front of big crowds. With the reserves playing in midweek I go along and watch the first team on Saturdays but it sickens me when I think I could be down on the pitch with them."

Although he regained his fitness sufficiently to play another couple of reserve team games in February and March, with the Rangers first team running away with Division Two without his assistance, Currie was all too aware that his contract (which was due to expire in June 1983) would not be renewed.

"I haven't had any talks with the manager yet," Tony stated in February, "but with the team doing so well without me I don't see much of a future at Loftus Road. I would love to stay and play in the First Division, but the way things have gone I will probably be on my way."

As Rangers edged ever closer to a return to the First Division (they were eventually promoted as champions of Division Two, ten points clear of second placed Wolves), Currie summarily received the news that he had been dreading: "Terry Venables came to me one day and said my contract was up and that [Jim] Gregory didn't want to keep me on. I didn't realise that they should at least have offered me another year."

Currie had managed only 81 league appearances in four seasons for Rangers, and, while the string of injuries he suffered during his time at Loftus Road prevented him from writing his name into QPR folklore in the same way that Rodney Marsh and Stanley Bowles had, he remains fondly remembered by his Hoops team-mates and the club's fans for his range of passing and his repertoire of tricks.

"When Terry Venables was manager in the 80s, I'd say that was the best team I've ever played in," defender Steve Wicks reflects. "[And] the greatest player I ever played with was Tony Currie. He really knew how to put a shift in and represented everything that QPR stood for."

"Tony was fantastic," QPR diehard Dave Thomas genuflects. "You run out of superlatives for these players.

The number 10 shirt at QPR is legendary, and Tony Currie filled it admirably in the same way that Simon Stainrod did later. They [Marsh, Bowles, Currie and Stainrod] were the four players that really deserved it. Currie was right up there with Marsh and Bowles in terms of showmanship and ability and fitting that famous shirt. The only difference is that Currie didn't play nearly enough for us. He was a wonderful player – he had as many tricks as Bowles or Marsh. If you say that Bowles and Marsh were Man United and Liverpool, then Currie was Aston Villa or Leeds. Slightly behind those two, but still spoken of in reverential terms and with a great deal of affection."

* * * * *

On 29th April, on Venables' recommendation, and for a cut-price transfer fee of £40,000 (a tenth what QPR had paid Leeds), Currie flew to Canada to sign a five-month contract reportedly worth £11,000 with Toronto Nationals – one of the founder members of the inaugural Canadian Professional Soccer League.

"I thought I could have five months of competitive soccer with the Nationals during the summer season," Tony stated, explaining his reasons for accepting the move, "to reach peak fitness and then hopefully return [to England] to find a new club."

Kicking off in May 1983, the CPSL was the first attempt to establish a truly national and professional league in Canada. The league would consist of six teams: Hamilton Steelers (winners of Canada's 1981 semi-pro National Soccer League championship), Mississauga Croatia SC (who had existed in some form since 1977), and four franchises formed specifically to compete in this new league: Edmonton Eagles, Inter-Montreal FC,

Calgary Mustangs and Toronto Nationals. The clubs were scheduled to play a 30-game season and, in a bid to encourage home-grown talent, a Canadian content rule was imposed restricting each club to five imports per team.

With the exception of Inter-Montreal (whose sponsorship deal with Labatt's Brewery meant they could afford a clutch of "name" imports – among them highly decorated Greek international midfielder Takis Nikoloudis (signed from AEK Athens), Yugoslav international Raddy Avramovic fresh from four seasons in England with Notts County, former Italian international sweeper Pino Wilson, former Dutch international midfielder Robert Vosmaer and former Manchester United and England winger Gordon Hill), the other CPSL teams were largely staffed by a mixture of unattached former NASL players, those on hiatus from the Major Indoor Soccer League and various Canadian amateur leagues. The presence of Currie, then, was therefore somewhat anomalous for the CPSL, as was the size of his transfer fee; a fact not lost on the man who would be his new coach – ex-Plymouth Argyle midfielder and former coach of the Canadian Olympic Soccer team, Frank Pike.

"Currie cost a fair bit of dough," Pike admitted. "He's a very skilful and colourful player. But he's been told clearly that he has to assist in the development of Canadian players. Or don't bother coming."

Despite this rather unnecessary broadside Currie was initially excited to be part of an initiative aimed at promoting the game in what was, after all, a footballing backwater. "There are many minor leagues in Canada but when players reach a certain level there is no further incentive," Tony told *Shoot!* "By forming a professional league young players will be inclined to think about making a career out of the game."

At first everything seemed to be shaping up nicely. Although many miles from home, Tony had no difficulties settling in, a process helped by the fact he would serendipitously be joining up with former team-mate Colin Franks who had been playing in the North American Soccer League since February 1979, firstly for Toronto Blizzard and latterly for the Edmonton Drillers prior to his move to the Nationals.

"I was lucky to have Colin Franks in the team," Currie remarked, "an ex-team-mate from earlier Watford and Sheffield United days who [was] resident in Canada and a very good friend of mine. He made the settling-in process very easy."

Although the club's management failed in a much-publicised bid to add Polish legend Grzegorz Lato to their roster, the Nationals did have enough useful players – among them experienced German defender Hans-Gunter Neues (who had recently been released by FC Kaiserslautern), Canadian international Frank Ciaccia and Ecuadorian international Carlos Torres Garces as well as Currie and Franks – to look forward to the season with a good degree of optimism.

The much ballyhooed CPSL finally got under way on 21st May when Toronto entertained Inter-Montreal. Although a near sell-out crowd of 20,500 had been predicted at Varsity Stadium, a mere fraction of that figure was there to witness the Nationals emerge 2-1 winners thanks to goals from Franks (set up by Currie) and Croatian midfielder Slavko Petrina.

Six days later the Nationals continued their fine start to the season, holding eventual champions Edmonton Eagles to a creditable 1-1 draw, and, on 3rd June, in their third game of the campaign, they beat Mississauga Croatia 3-0 to climb to second in the table.

Playing as a striker in the latter match Currie had opened the scoring in the 66th minute with what was described by *The Calgary Herald* as, "a shot from 35 metres that cleanly beat Mississauga goalie Dale Baxter."

"We had great leadership from Tony Currie, who played very well," the Nationals' general manager / coach Frank Pike beamed (the other two goals coming from Torres Garces). "He generaled the attack and started the flood."

"I was playing as a striker tonight," Currie patiently explained to the *Herald*. "That's probably why I got a few more shots, but I don't know if I'm going to continue at striker – I've been a midfield player for 14 years."

Despite the Nationals' unbeaten start to the season, things quickly began to turn sour. Although Currie and his team-mates were beaten 4-2 in their return fixture with bottom-of-the-table Mississauga Croatia on 5th June, their first defeat of the season was the least of their concerns.

It would later emerge that the players had not been paid since 15th May and it was soon being widely reported, just four games into the season, that the club was on the verge of extinction.

Despite reportedly frittering more than $200,000 of its purported $1million operating budget trying to market the team, the club had suffered badly at the turnstiles. With average gates of 1,000 falling some considerable way short of the 5,000 spectators needed to break even, on 10th June the club's majority owner and president John Welton abruptly departed, stating that he wanted nothing more to do with the Toronto Nationals.

According to Colin Franks' memories that the players were annoyed and worried about their livelihoods is putting it mildly: "Frank Pike told us the money was gone so I said, 'We are not playing.' He said we would all be suspended so I said that would last a week and then we would be free agents as we had not been paid."

Although the players would remain with the team in the short term general manager/coach Frank Pike would not. In the face of the club's financial difficulties Pike opted to desert the sinking ship, resigning shortly after the announcement of Welton's departure.

With the team placed under league trusteeship and Colin Franks now acting as team coach, the players held a meeting on 10th June to decide what to do next. Although disbanding was seriously considered, at the end of the meeting most of the players, Currie included, agreed to continue playing without pay in the hope that a new owner could be found.

Having agreed to continue the team travelled west to face league leaders Edmonton on 12th June. Although they put up stubborn resistance in a narrow 2-1 loss, by the following Wednesday when they visited Calgary, that fight had evidently been extinguished, as they capitulated to a 4-0 humbling. To cap a miserable week, with his frustrations getting the better of him, Currie was sent off in the second half for swearing at the referee (a particular bug bear of CPSL referees, who according to Colin Franks, were simply not used to it). It would be his last CPSL appearance.

"The Toronto Nationals dressing room resembled a morgue Wednesday night," Mario Toneguzzi staff writer for *The Calgary Herald,* sympathised. "The players were not so much upset with a 4-0 thrashing at the hands of the Calgary Mustangs, but they were bitter with their CPSL team's management. The Nationals are on the brink of extinction and the players' emotions have been of frustration, bitterness and betrayal as well as a sense of bewilderment."

"With the problems we have, I don't see us playing past tonight," bemoaned Nationals goalkeeper John Baretta, clearly speaking for all of his colleagues. "We find out Friday what happens. I know I for one won't play anymore for nothing.

"We've been playing like this since we beat Mississauga 3-0 at home. We've been going downhill. We've been losing because of that. It's difficult for anyone to play not knowing if and when we'll be getting a pay cheque. It's indicative of the way we played today. The frustrations off the field are showing on the field.

"A lot of us have families," added Baretta. "What do we do now? It's been so frustrating the whole thing. I've never had this feeling in my whole life. It is a feeling of despair – of not knowing whether there will be a team to play for tomorrow when the players arrive in Toronto."

Unfortunately for Currie and his team-mates, Baretta's fears were proved to be correct and, on Friday 17th June, the Toronto Nationals *officially* folded.

There would be one final twist in the Nationals saga, however, when, the following day, it was announced that the club had been purchased by a group of unnamed private investors (believed to include the Toronto-based MTV).

The club's former marketing manager and new general manager Jack Kligman told the press that the new club would assume its predecessor's schedule but would not have a team name until legal proceedings determined whether it could use the Nationals' moniker.

"The new owners know what is needed to make the franchise viable," Kligman vowed but warned that while the original Nationals players would be invited to stay with the new team, their salaries would have to be renegotiated, that is to say slashed.

For Tony this was the last straw: "The stress upon me and the other players in the side over the last month left me disillusioned, and a cut in wages was just not acceptable. Understandably, most of the Canadian players have remained, but thinking of the future, I thought it would be wiser for me to return home."

This turned out to be a shrewd decision. Although it appears that the new team did complete one more fixture (sporting the same kit but shorn of both their nickname and their star players, Currie and Neues, they lost 3-2 away at Hamilton on 26th June), the new backers hurriedly withdrew their offer to buy the team and the remaining players were left high and dry for the second time in a fortnight.

"The first month was good," Currie would later say of his time in Canada, which had seen him receive just two weeks' pay, "the second month was a nightmare."

As with every other attempt in North America to sell soccer to the masses the CPSL enterprise had been doomed to ignominious failure from the start. The organisation was shambolic, the marketing of the league was poor and reporting of fixtures and results was haphazard and often contradictory depending on which newspaper you read. In addition, several of the owners simply did not have the cash to support the running of a football club and as a result payment of players' wages was sporadic even at the supposedly better-run and solvent clubs and indifferent fans stayed away in their droves, because, ultimately, there was little indigenous mass appetite for association football in Canada.

Toronto Nationals may have been the first to fold but they were followed quickly by Inter-Montreal (perhaps it was no coincidence that Toronto and Montreal each already had operating soccer clubs – Toronto Blizzard and Montreal Manic – neither of whom were plying their trade in the NASL in the rudest of health) and Calgary Mustangs only survived a similar fate on 16th June when they were bailed out by a wealthy, local, soccer-mad family.

Despite the loss of two of its founder members the CPSL remarkably attempted to continue, with the remaining clubs doing their best to fulfil the defunct clubs' fixtures.

In July lip service was still being paid to the notion that Montreal and Toronto might find the new investors that would allow them to resume CPSL participation and although a group headed by Inter's captain Bob Vosmaer and businessman Tony Iammatteo did arrive with a rescue package to bail out the former, Iammatteo's conditions for investing were simple and two-fold: firstly that Toronto Nationals also find new backers and secondly that he received a guarantee that the CPSL would continue to operate.

With Toronto unable to find new owners, therefore effectively putting the kibosh on Montreal's resurrection, the CPSL decided on 12th July to halt the league, announcing that it would attempt to salvage something from the wreckage by having the four remaining teams compete in a make shift best-of-three semi-final play-off.

For the record in the play-off final on 1st August Edmonton Eagles beat Hamilton Steelers 2-0. Following this the Canadian Professional Soccer League was not only done and dusted but gone for good, consigned to history as little more than a football statistician's footnote.

* * * * *

Currie returned home from his ill-fated Canadian sojourn to find himself unemployed. Incredibly, despite the fact that he was only 33 years of age, hardly over the hill even for a midfielder, and barely a year after appearing in the 1982 FA Cup Final, no Football League club seemed willing to give him a game.

With no offers from a Football League club on the table, Tony found himself slumming it in the second tier of the Isthmian League for Chesham United, a small Buckinghamshire outfit captained by his brother, Paul. Surely a man of Currie's talents deserved better than this!

One person who evidently agreed was Sheffield United chairman Reg Brealey who offered Tony a three-month contract.

Inevitably rumours of Tony's prodigal return reached the Bramall Lane faithful, who, in eager anticipation, proceeded to vociferously sing his name on the terraces during United's 4-0 win over Gillingham, which, incidentally, apparently so incensed the Blades' current idol Keith Edwards that the striker was inspired to bag all four goals.

"There was talk of Currie coming back to the club," Edwards later explained, "which was exciting for me because that would have been great. I'd loved to have seen him come back, even though he was in the late stages of his career. But, being competitive, when the fans were chanting Currie's name, I felt it was a little disrespectful to me and it gave me the gee-up that I probably needed… I thought, 'They're not singing for an old player while I'm on that field. I want them to sing for me.'"

Regrettably though, when Currie met with then United manager, the late Ian Porterfield, it was clear that he was not part of the manager's plans.

"Sheffield United more or less agreed wages," Currie explained, "but I got the impression that Ian Porterfield might have regarded me as a threat, so I saved him any problems and decided not to go. Then Ken Bates called me up and said he wanted me to work with the reserves at Chelsea [where ironically his old rival Alan Hudson was then also trying to resurrect his career after a spell in North America]. I can't remember whether he said he would contact me or vice versa, but neither of us did. I wasn't bothered, which wasn't like me at all. I must have been in a bad way."

Faced with Currie's injury problems and the risks involved in subjecting his left knee in particular to further punishment, most pros would have simply hung up their boots and bought a nice little pub or found a comfy chair behind a radio mike. Such was Tony's love of the game, however, that he was determined to carry on until the body finally said no more.

The PFA covered the cost of a series of knee operations, which enabled Currie to sign for Southend on a three-month trial basis. It turned out to be an unmitigated disaster. Preparing to make his debut at Roots Hall Tony somehow contrived to get injured running out of the tunnel! Hobbling back to the dressing room he broke the news to the manager Peter Morris who, according to Currie, went ballistic: "He was chuckin' things about and swearing!"

The touchline injury sidelined Currie for six weeks. Although he recovered sufficiently to make two demeaning appearances for the Shrimpers' reserves, when his trial period expired, Morris told Currie his services were no longer required.

Southend's loss proved to be the gain of Fourth Division Torquay United, for whom Tony was persuaded to sign in February by his old mate, David Webb, who was then in charge at Plainmoor. Webb offered Tony the following shibboleth: "Come down Friday night, play Saturday and do your bit on the pitch."

Currie made his debut at home to Northampton on 3rd March 1984 – Tony's first taste of the Football League since 13th November 1982 – in front of less than 2,000 spectators. For the next game against York City the gate had swelled to almost 3,000.

Although Currie's presence did have a positive effect on the box-office receipts, it seemed there was little he could do to change Torquay's stolidly mid-table fortunes on the pitch. Currie played in nine of Torquay's last 15 league games that season, resulting in a Shanghai of three wins, three defeats and three draws. Torquay, who were tenth when Currie arrived in March, finished the season in ninth place.

The following season, Currie added another seven league and cup games to his Torquay stats. Although Currie did notch the winner against Hereford early in November (his last ever league goal – fittingly a spectacular long-range screamer), it was an isolated highlight. Indeed of the seven games he played during the 1984-85 season, Tony was on the losing side five times. At the end of the season Torquay United finished the season bottom of the Fourth Division, grateful that automatic relegation to the Conference would not be introduced until 1986-87.

While Currie still had the class, he *was* past his best and the fact that he was carrying a few extra pounds, coupled with a diminution of pace, left him at the mercy of the agricultural tackles that remain a feature of the lower reaches of the Football League. It was clear that the left knee could only take so much punishment and on 1st December 1984, Currie played his 528th and last Football League game – a 3-1 defeat away at Bury in front of just 2,600 hardy perennials.

One week later, on 8th December, Tony played his last ever game as a professional footballer, away at Leyton

Orient in the FA Cup second round. Unfortunately a crushing 3-0 Orient win prevented Tony ending his distinguished playing career with a win.

As with all his clubs, and despite the brevity of his stay on the south coast, Tony left the Plainmoor faithful with plenty of indelible memories.

"I have wonderful memories of Tony Currie's time at Torquay United," recalls Gulls fan Alex Campbell. "He was a master on the ball, such composure, he could control the game with such ease and what a dead ball specialist, his free kicks were absolutely lethal, such power and accuracy, he was a pleasure to watch."

Now that he was effectively robbed of his livelihood, Tony Currie stood at the crossroads facing a highly uncertain future. Although he was not inundated with job offers that would have kept him in the game, one invitation Currie did receive was to become the manager of Wigan Athletic.

"After I packed in playing I never thought about managing, although I wish I had now," Tony states. "I did have the chance to go to Wigan once. One of the directors who used to be at Sheffield [Tony Barrington] ended up as their chairman and he asked me to be their player-manager. But I'd just got divorced and I didn't want to leave the children. I didn't want to leave London, and Wigan seemed like a thousand miles away."

As a result, and much to his later regret, Currie decided to turn it down. "Wigan were in the lower divisions in those days, but it would have been a start. It's a big regret because I should have taken it. I would have been about 34 or 35 and who knows what would have happened. I could have ended up being England manager! You never know how things would have worked out and that's down to the fact that I didn't take the bloody chance."

Instead, presumably against sound medical advice, Currie opted to continue playing. With no league clubs willing to take a punt on an ageing, crocked schemer, Tony fished for a game around the non-leagues. It says a great deal about Currie that despite a shot knee, he made every possible effort to keep playing. His quest was not financially motivated; it was pure love of the game.

"After Torquay, I ended up playing non-league football in the south for Hendon, Finchley and Dunstable. I basically played for anybody who wanted to give me a game." With his left knee now screaming for him to quit, Tony finally decided to hang up his boots – at least temporarily.

At this point Tony headed back to London to live in his mum's council house with his brother and two uncles. With most of his £400 monthly pension eaten up by maintenance payments to his ex-wife and three children, Sharon, Ryan and Natalie, to whom he naturally wished to remain near, Currie had no other choice. "I wasn't living with my kids who were four miles away. I was left with hardly anything after the divorce settlement and from 1983 to 1988, I was just messing about, not doing much really. I had to look after my kids, so to make ends meet I did odd jobs here and there."

After a short-lived spell working in a video shop Currie took up minicabbing; a two-month experiment that ended when the car blew up!

Despite being unemployed, pride prevented Tony from signing on the dole. "I'm an impatient person and I hate queues," he remarks, "but I also never thought of it as my entitlement." It was, as Currie concedes, "a very difficult time."

Professional sport is littered with individuals who find it difficult to adjust to life after retirement. Many find the emotional difficulties of transitioning to life after fame and success, and the challenges of finding a new purpose once their career is over too onerous, and many, like Currie, find solace in drink.

"I was very depressed," Tony openly admits. "I had a room at my mum's but I became a bit of a recluse. I didn't have a drinking problem, but like most people do when things like that happen I was drinking a lot. I have always been a bit of a home bird, but things were so bad that I never went out. Most days I would just be up in my room watching television with a bottle. My family were very worried and did everything they could to help. But I felt very lonely. Things were bad and a lot of people in football were worried about me as well as my family."

Tony has admitted that it was not out of the ordinary for him to get through four bottles of whisky a week, although he has always vehemently denied that he was ever an alcoholic.

"I'd lost my wife and my career and I didn't have a job," he states. "I was 33 years old and on the scrap heap. It was really 1983 when my drinking got bad, but I wasn't hooked. I'd do a bottle one day and then not touch the bloody stuff the next. I never wanted to see it again, but then after a day off I'd have some more. I was drinking to forget what was happening. I suppose that's why most people drink. It wasn't a problem, though. You drink to put things out of your mind and that's fine. I wasn't addicted. It wasn't that hard for me to get off it."

It wasn't long before the tabloids found out that the great Tony Currie, arguably the finest midfield playmaker of his generation, was on his uppers. When *The Sun* newspaper duly tracked him down and induced him to pour his heart out, it was clear that Currie's reduced financial circumstances had little to do with improvidence but was due rather more to a failure to maximise his earning potential throughout a professional career that had spanned almost 20 years – a situation that would be unthinkable in the present-day era.

"I should have made a fortune out of football," Currie told *The Sun* in 1986, "but I have always been naïve and immature where money is concerned. When I was at the height of my career I saw how contemporaries like Kevin Keegan got themselves agents and worked hard at making money. I never bothered with all that. I was stupid enough to believe that I did not have to provide for the future because I thought I could play the game I love forever. Now I'm paying the price for being so gullible."

Although Tony was fortunately able to find the willpower to moderate his drinking habits, his future circa 1986 remained uncertain. Although another knee operation had offered cause for optimism, the surgery was not a success.

A week after the operation, Tony found himself unable to walk and poison had to be drained from the troublesome knee a month later.

What Tony Currie did not know at that stage was that salvation was just around the corner in the shape of two testimonial matches at Bramall Lane.

After an appearance in Tony Kenworthy's testimonial in May 1986 (following which Tony met his second wife, Jane), word quickly got about that the former Blades idol could do with a lift, both financially and psychologically.

A testimonial was quickly organised for Tony by a committee that included his good friend and former team-mate Len Badger, and, on Sunday 5th October 1986 almost 18,000 fans turned up at Bramall Lane to watch their idol play that day for a Sheffield United all-star side versus a Dennis Waterman Showbiz XI. 18,000, incidentally, represented the Lane's biggest gate of the season!

The crowd that day gave Tony a prodigal son's reception. "It was the most moving day of my life," Currie recalls. "They'd all turned up for me."

Waterman's XI boasted the likes of George Best, Allan Clarke, Billy Bremner, Geoff Hurst, Roy McFarland, Frank Worthington, Archie Gemmill, comedian Mick Miller and Def Leppard vocalist Joe Elliott, who flew in especially from Holland. "I would have swum all the way to be here," Elliott bubbled. "Tony is my hero. I rate him above any rock star."

Currie, meanwhile, was able to attract old mates (and former Blades) Alan Birchenall and Ken Mallender and the entire Sheffield United 1970-71 promotion-winning side, including Tulsa-based Alan Woodward, whose trip "home" was financed by local people and businesses.

For the Class of '71 it was just like old times: "It was like we'd never been apart," recalls Len Badger, describing the dressing room atmosphere. "When you've shared what we had, you didn't have to say anything."

"The emphasis will be on skill and entertainment," Tony had promised before the game, "something that's sadly lacking nowadays," and the match didn't disappoint, finishing in a 7-5 victory for the former Blades (with the Blades' goals, for the record, coming from Billy Dearden (3), Woodward (2), Eddie Colquhoun and Geoff Salmons).

Living up to his pre-match theme tune, 'You Can Do Magic', Currie, despite the impediment of a heavily bandaged left knee, rolled back the years, treating the fans to a vintage display of inch-perfect passes and showmanship that was marred only by a spot kick miss (fortuitously saved by Mick Miller's legs). At the final whistle, an emotional day was rounded off when hordes of jubilant fans mobbed Currie as he left the field.

"It was wonderful," Tony says. "A great day. The stadium was packed. I was playing football and amongst friends. I couldn't have asked for anything more."

"The whole thing was unbelievable," Howard Stephenson of Tony's testimonial committee added for good measure, "the attendance, the atmosphere, the pop groups and the soccer stars… This is the way football should be. We were looking for around 10,000 but such was the overflow we opened the Bramall Lane stand to cope. We printed only 3,000 programmes and they were a sell-out and are now a collectors' item. Tony himself still can't believe the support. He finished legless and still hasn't got his voice back."

As Currie himself admitted, the testimonial game (from which he was reputed to have pocketed £25,000) was, "the start of me getting back on my feet."

Having returned to Sheffield to help organise his testimonial and the various events that surrounded it, Tony made the decision to move back permanently. Within a year he and Jane were married.

There was even more good news to come in the shape of yet another knee operation (this one involving a series of holes being drilled into the problem area). At first, the operation appeared to have been a complete success.

"It used to balloon to twice its normal size," says Tony. "[The] operation in 1987 … seemed to cure it and, like a pillock, I thought I'd be all right to play again. Worst thing I could do. But no one said don't do it."

In October 1987, Currie, now 37, pitched up at Goole Town, then in the Northern Premier League, managed by his old pal and ex-Sheffield United team-mate Paddy Buckley.

Currie made his Town debut against Buxton on 7th October and he showed that he'd lost none of his class in masterminding an unlikely comeback for his new team who had found themselves trailing 3-1 with only 20 minutes remaining.

"Currie saw little of the ball for most of the game," purred *The Green 'Un*, "but when his new team-mates started giving him possession he began to dominate the midfield and put Goole on the victory trail with a series of defence splitting passes."

Courtesy of Currie's undimmed vision Goole scored three times in the last quarter to win 4-3 with the winning goal coming in the last minute.

Three days later Currie was again pulling the strings as Goole ran out 3-1 winners at home to Rhyl and rolled back the years for a third time in a week by capping a stupendous second half display with a stunning goal in Town's 3-0 win away at Gainsborough Trinity. Marooned in the bottom half of the table before he arrived, Currie's precision passing and overall influence on his team-mates had helped propel Goole to fourth in the league and there was soon talk that 1987-88 could finally be the East Yorkshire side's year.

"The magical skills of Tony Currie," predicted *The Green 'Un,* have inspired Goole Town so much that manager Paddy Buckley's talented side looks capable of chasing their first ever Northern Premier League championship."

Unfortunately, Goole's good fortune wouldn't last when after nine more games (and one more goal in Town's 3-1 defeat to Morecambe in the GMAC Cup quarter-final replay), Currie's knee went for the last time. After 20 years in the game it was finally time to hang up the boots. Naturally, Tony was devastated.

"I'm the type who would have gone on and on," he admitted, "I'd still be playing Sunday League football now if my left knee was as good as my right because you can't replace playing the game. I can't ride a bike or jog now because I'd be in a chair for three weeks."

Despite the brevity of his time in the East Riding of Yorkshire, he remains fondly remembered by those who saw him in the twilight of his playing days.

"Tony Currie only played for about three months with the club," recalls *Goole Times* football correspondent Graeme Wilson, "but it was great to have him playing on the Victoria Pleasure Grounds. He scored twice I recall from memory – the most memorable in a 3-0 win at Gainsborough Trinity in the Northern Premier League where he struck a volley from all of 25 yards from a corner played back deep to him on purpose – just unbelievable technique and out of the top drawer.

"His other goal came in a GMAC Cup tie at Morecambe. Nothing major there, except on the way home the team coach broke down at Lancaster, and the landlord of the Skerton Arms couldn't believe that a coach with the legend that was Tony Currie on board, could break down 50 yards from his pub. He turfed out his regulars at closing time, and allowed us in with Tony, who recited stories about his career, until a replacement coach picked us up from Selby at 2am – we got home at 4.30am – priceless and drunk!"

* * * * *

Although his playing days were now behind him, Tony was, perhaps unsurprisingly, keen to stay in the game. Regrettably, although he did apply for several managerial positions, Tony was unable to find a club chairman prepared to take a punt on his abilities, that would forever remain unproven.

"I applied for the Rotherham job before Ronnie Moore got it and I also applied for the job at Shrewsbury," Currie recalls. "But I didn't get an interview for either position."

"I also put in for the Sheffield United job twice – before Dave Bassett and after he was in charge – but that was only under pressure from friends. Fans were writing to the local paper saying I should be the manager so I felt obliged to apply. I didn't expect to get it and perhaps didn't really want it, so I wasn't disappointed when I didn't get a reply."

Fortunately the footballing tooth fairies ensured Tony would find a niche within the game he loved so much and at the club where he had made his name.

* * * * *

The Football in the Community project was first established as part of the Footballers' Further Education & Vocational Training Society Limited (FFE & VTS) and continues to operate with the full support of the Football Association, the FA Premier League, the Football League and the Professional Footballers' Association.

According to the FITC website, "The ultimate intention was to develop links so that clubs forged a meaningful relationship within the local community."

After a successful pilot scheme in 1986 in the North West of England (involving Manchester City, Bolton Wanderers, Bury, Manchester United, Oldham Athletic and Preston North End), in early 1988, the scheme was expanded to include the clubs based in Yorkshire, the North East and the Midlands.

Naturally that meant a position as Football in the Community officer was available at Sheffield United and, with Tony back living in the North, he was the obvious candidate.

"I heard about this job – this would have been in 1987," Currie recalls, "and I think the club had more or less earmarked me for it, but I went through the formal procedure of applying for it and started in February 1988."

"Funnily enough, I started work on 1st February, which was exactly 20 years to the day after I actually signed for United."

Currie was thrilled to be given the opportunity to pass on his skills and enthusiasm for the game: "I felt very fortunate to be getting up in the mornings and going to work at a club where I'd had such happy times... I love Sheffield, the people, the place, the fans, everything about it and I was delighted to get back into football at the Lane."

The job was no sinecure, though. Indeed, following his appointment, Tony remarkably found himself faced with the considerable challenge of having to build up his new role from scratch.

"All I really knew was that the job was to involve the whole community," Tony attested in 1995, "from senior citizens down to schoolkids, the unemployed, ethnic groups, everybody. We were thrown in at the deep end, really! We had nothing down on paper. It was a case of going out and looking for the work, ringing schools, approaching the education departments.

"At first people were very sceptical. It was hard work to bring them round. I was lucky, I suppose, in that most of the teachers knew me from my playing days. It was probably harder for other people doing the same job elsewhere who didn't have a 'big name' ... At first, United weren't too sure about what we were up to either."

Although Tony's job would involve organising all sorts of events such as bingo, trips to Scarborough and tea dances for the elderly, the primary focus of his new role would be capturing the hearts and minds of the schoolchildren who, it was hoped, would become the next generation of Sheffield United supporters.

Tony and his assistants would visit two schools a day where they would host a training session and invite the children to come for a tour of Bramall Lane, which in turn would be followed by an invitation to attend a match.

"I have a staff of six employment training workers with me," Tony elaborated in 1989. "They go to college on Thursdays and that's when I organise school visits to the ground. In the morning the children are shown around the ground, meet the police and see the police horses. Then, in the afternoon, they do school work at the ground involving tasks such as measuring distances and angles, writing and initiative tests. I feel like a schoolteacher, football coach, administrator and accountant."

With staff to supervise, manage and assess and mountains of paperwork to plough through, in addition to organising events, the job was never short of pressures. After "20 years of kicking a football about", Tony admitted that he initially found it difficult to cope with these demands. It says much for his enthusiasm and appetite for hard work that he made such a success of the role, quickly turning it into a self-supporting operation and earning himself in the process an entirely new generation of fans.

"The kids go home and tell their parents they've had a visit to their school from Tony Currie and the mums and dads tell them all about me. I drive around in the Football in the Community minibus and I get youngsters waving at me in the street. It's just like the old days really."

Although he left the role of United's Football in the Community officer in 2008 to take up a position at United's impressive academy in Shirecliffe, Tony can be justifiably proud of his role in the programme's success.

"[At the start] we didn't get paid, we had to generate our own funding," Currie recalled in 2014. "But we did it because we loved the club. Back then, we used to work with the unemployed to help them get coaching badges and among the first was Tony Minichello who, as everyone knows, went on to become Jess Ennis's coach. He quite clearly had a knack for the job, didn't he? Another thing we did to generate our funding was birthday parties and training camps. I still get people coming up now saying they remember having one of those so goodness knows how many fans we helped create."

* * * * *

Nothing, though, can replace the thrill of playing the game, but because of Tony's injured knee, even his occasional outings in charity matches can leave him in a lot of pain.

"I played so often when I was injured that there is little doubt that I kept aggravating the problem," Tony says. "I liked to have the ball a lot and consequently took a lot of knocks.

"My love of playing meant that I tried to hide my injuries and often played when I shouldn't. I probably only played about five matches in my whole career when I was 100% fit. If I'd have been more careful I would probably have had a longer career. I'm sure such circumstances wouldn't be allowed today.

"Of course I miss playing," Tony continues. "Who wouldn't after the career I enjoyed in the game? The knee just won't stand up to it any more. Injuries are a lot to do with luck. Some players can go through a tough professional career and have no problems when they retire. I suppose I've just not been so lucky, but I can't grumble.

I'm having a great time with what I'm doing now... I've been hitting the targets I've wanted to hit and I am my own boss. It's brilliant."

Although Currie's job is high profile within Sheffield, he has kept a low profile on the national scene. While many former pros can often be found joining in the enervating banter on *A Question of Sport* or sitting in the Sky studios watching closed circuit television of Premiership matches, Currie is rarely, if ever, seen on our television screens (although he did appear on a celebrity edition of the quiz show *Eggheads* in December 2011 alongside Kerry Dixon, Alan Kennedy, Alan Rough and Frank Worthington). But then, Currie was never that comfortable in front of the cameras, as anyone who saw his cameo in the 1996 film *When Saturday Comes* alongside Blades fanatic Sean Bean (a tall tale about a brewery worker who overcame the booze to hit the big time with Sheffield United) would endorse.

Despite the riches on offer in the modern game, Currie remains happy to have played when he did, aware perhaps that the modern game has little or no place for his sort of player, the sort of player whose instincts were, first and foremost, to *entertain* the paying public.

"The game has changed," laments John Motson. It's so fast. Stan Bowles or Tony Currie couldn't sit on the ball now; there's no time for craftsmanship, embroidery on the ball or a bit of fun. We've lost that. This is the Patrick Vieira generation; players just help the ball on. Midfield play is about athletes and aggression."

That football is now primarily a business rather than an entertainment needs hardly be reiterated. The stakes are simply too high to take risks. The cost of defeat and relegation has ensured that pragmatism reigns over style and aesthetics. The maverick, fun-loving, romantic, stylish element epitomised by Currie *et al* has been phased, even driven out.

"Everyone says the game's better and players are fitter now, but I can't see it," Currie asserts. "We used to have to trudge through inches of mud from November. They don't do that now and they don't go back in the afternoons and run their wotsits off. Now all the pitches are like Wembley and the players don't have to worry if it's going to hit a bobble. Players are already looking ahead, so they've got improved vision and skills. In my day there were a handful of players in the entire league who were good enough to know what they were going to do with the ball before they got it – and I was one of them. Now it's all special diets and personal trainers, but that's just show. What people forget is that it's easier running on grass than ploughing through sludge."

Since the retirements of Paul Gascoigne, Chris Waddle and Matt Le Tissier, England no longer have an out-and-out midfield schemer worthy of the name.

"That's the big difference between the game then and the game today," Tony concurs. "Football was played with a smile in those days. Now, because of the pressure put on modern players and managers, it's played with a frown. Football for me was a game to be enjoyed. It was a privilege to be a professional footballer and, while I didn't make a fortune out of the game, I don't regret a thing. Because of the way people like me and…so many other characters that were around in the 1970s approached the game, I doubt we would survive minutes today. Referees have no sense of humour these days and there's no way they would stand for some of the things we got up to. We would have had to change our act and probably not been half the players. I couldn't have gone through my career not having a laugh and trying things on. I would have packed it all in."

"The big high for me was playing every week. I couldn't wait to get out there and show people what I could do. I loved it."

Currie, now remarried for a third time to Elizabeth and a grandfather, remains fiercely proud of his achievements in the game: "I got more caps than the likes of Bowles, Hudson, Marsh and Worthington. I also played 12 times at Wembley and there are lots of players who never played there at all.

"People say I never achieved what I should have done, but I actually achieved exactly what I wanted to. OK, I'd have liked to play 100 times for England but that was out of my hands. People got a hell of a lot of pleasure from seeing me play and I've still got the letters to prove it."

Certainly the absence of a cabinet bulging with England caps and winners' medals don't dilute by a single drop of soda, Tony Currie's contribution to the sport he continues to serve.

"Tony Currie is one of the best players I've ever known," testified the late Alan Woodward (who died earlier this year on 21st May 2015), "he was absolutely unreal and I couldn't believe some of the things he used to do – he used to make me look good! The balls I used to get were absolutely tremendous, one touch and it would be in the net."

"Tony was absolutely some talent," Alan Hudson genuflects, "but he was the one that I always thought that I had to fight for a place with England. It just so happened that neither of us really played and it was just dumbfounding."

"He will go down as one of the most underrated footballers who played the game," Rodney Marsh adds. "Because he could do it all."

"You couldn't value him in today's market," Ray Hankin eulogises. "He would be worth a hundred million and a truly great player. I treasured my time with Tony at Leeds as he was my room-mate, mate and a great, great player."

"Tony was a great player," Frank Worthington concludes, "really fantastic, and capable of doing things you only see players like Thierry Henry, Dennis Bergkamp or Gianfranco Zola try these days. Tony was my room-mate with England and I've always thought his initials said it all. TC: Top Class."

One only has to visit a fan forum on the internet dedicated to any of the clubs Currie played for to find hundreds of golden memories of his brilliance. My favourite is this one that I found on a Sheffield United forum that I think perfectly encapsulates the esteem and the idolatry in which he was held: "I was stood on the John Street Terrace on a really wet night, and there was a young boy at the front by the railings getting soaked to the skin. The ball went out of play for a United throw-in, TC went to collect it from near where the young boy stood. The boy said to our hero 'Tony, please make it stop raining.'"

Since the first edition of this book, not a great deal has changed. Tony is still at Sheffield United. After 20 years as the Blades' Football in the Community officer Currie worked at United's academy for three years, and is now employed by the club in an ambassadorial role. If anything, his new role is even more high profile.

"As club ambassador," Tony explains, "I go to shop openings, cut ribbons, give talks at hospitals, visit old peoples' homes and provide hospitality at Bramall Lane on matchdays.

"I went to a shop opening once and someone asked me to dribble down the street with a can of beans! It was hilarious. I did my best and managed to pull it off without breaking my foot.

"The ambassador role is a wonderful job," he continues. "It involves lots of different things but keeps me close to the heart of Sheffield United, which is important to me. I feel like part of the furniture now, I've been here that long. People think I'm from Yorkshire because I've lived in this part of the world for 34 years, even though I still got a strong London accent. It's great to be still working for United after 40 years. People know me very well although whenever I go to visit an old peoples' home no one seems to have a clue who I am, which makes a nice change.

"I still keep my hand in with summer coaching courses for kids in and around Sheffield. I find myself having to stand in for players at functions quite a lot when they can't make it for whatever reason. The club places a great emphasis on its role in the community so it's a busy job for me.

"The club is in my blood and I wouldn't have it any other way. I love entertaining people on matchdays. You get to see the game. But really I hate watching football. Nothing can ever replace that buzz of running out to entertain people. Now I have to entertain people off the pitch, but in my opinion it's not a bad replacement."

Memories of that ability to entertain people on the pitch though still live long in the minds of the fans and indeed everyone connected with Sheffield United.

In 2011 the club named a hospitality suite after him at Bramall Lane and dedicated a cabinet to him in the club museum and in September 2014 in a poll to celebrate the club's 125th anniversary, he was voted Sheffield United's greatest ever player – an award that left Tony struggling to find the right words to express his emotions when the award was presented to him at a special ceremony at Sheffield's Ponds Forge attended by his former team-mates Len Badger, Eddie Colquhoun, Ted Hemsley, and Alan Woodward.

"I didn't know what to say when it happened," Currie admitted. "Because I was choked, it meant so much. It's the most meaningful thing I've ever been given and I've been fortunate to collect some very treasured awards in recent times. I was so proud to represent England but, in a sense, this means more than those caps because it was voted for by the fans rather than just one man as it were."

It should be stressed that the esteem in which Tony is still held at Bramall Lane is very much a two-way street and after an association that now stretches back 46 years it is no surprise that Currie remains a Sheffield United fan at heart, and, like any supporter, longs to see the Blades back playing at the highest level.

"Our fans are the best in the business," Currie reckons. "This club means everything to me, it's my life, but it's those supporters that make it what it is. We've been in the third division for four seasons and 20,000 of them still turn up every week.

"I had a tear in my eye at Wembley," Currie admitted, when speaking of United's appearance in the FA Cup semi-final in April 2014. "I'll always remember walking to the stadium from the pub where we'd all gathered beforehand and it seemed like everyone wanted a picture which meant so much. Even more so, though, was the sight of us being back on that type of stage. The type of stage where, as far as I'm concerned, we belong.

"Before I get much older, I want to see us back in the big time. Let's go up and then do it again. Because that would be the greatest thing for me. It really, really would."

Selected Bibliography

Periodicals

Young Currie Takes His Chance – *Jimmy Hill's Football Weekly* (8th December 1967)

Tony Currie Interview – *Jimmy Hill's Football Weekly* (2nd August 1968)

Tony Currie – Youngster with So Much Skill – *Green 'Un* (28th September 1968)

I'm Shooting High But In Yorkshire You Can Make It – by Tony Currie – *Goal* (circa December 1968)

Expect Currie to Rocket Back to His Best – *Green 'Un* (12th November 1969)

Cockney Currie Is At Home In Sheffield – *Shoot!* (7th November 1970)

Our Attack Took the First Division by Surprise – by Tony Currie – *Goal* (23rd October 1971)

Bargain Buys – by Warwick Jordan – *Goal* (circa November 1971)

Hot Stuff This Currie – by Chris Coleman – *Striker* (15th January 1972)

Hot Stuff at Sheffield United – *Marshall Cavendish Book of Football Part 58* (circa 1972)

We Have More Shocks In Store – by Tony Currie – *Charles Buchan's Football Annual 1973*

The British Gunther Netzer… That's Tony Currie – *Goal* (circa 1973)

Two Targets For Tony Currie – *Shoot!* (24th August 1974)

Tony Currie's Secret Fear – *Shoot!* (7th December 1974)

My Route To The Top – by Tony Currie – *Billy Bremner's Book of Soccer 1974*

My Inspiration – by Tony Currie – *FA Book for Boys 26th Edition*

Starting Young – by Tony Currie – *Boys' Book of Soccer 1975*

My Perfect Volley – by Tony Currie – *Shoot! Annual 1975*

United Will Win Something – by Tony Currie – *Shoot!* (6th September 1975)

The Sad, Last Farewell – by Tony Pritchett – *Sheffield Star* (9th June 1976)

Tony's Last Lane Call – by Ian Vickers – *Sheffield Star* (9th June 1976)

The Phone Call I'm Waiting For – by Tony Currie – *Shoot!* (30th October 1976)

You Haven't Seen The Best of Me – *Shoot!* (11th June 1977)

Pro File: Tony Currie – *Football Handbook* (circa 1978)

Currie: Showman Who Added Effort – *Football Monthly* (February 1978)

The Brilliant Leopard Who Has Changed His Spots – *Sunday Times* (22nd October 1978)

Tony Currie Ace of Skills – *Soccer Monthly* (November 1978)

Tony Currie – Glad To Be Back in Town – *Shoot!* (29th September 1979)

Currie's Sentimental Journey – *Shoot!* (8th December 1979)

QPR's Magic Carpet – *Match Weekly* (11th July 1981)

Currie's Playing Better than Ever – *Shoot!* (18th July 1981)

Currie: A Danger To Spurs – *Shoot!* (29th May 1982)

Will Tony Turn It On? – *Shoot!* (29th May 1982)

Currie Set To Go – *Shoot!* (19th February 1983)

Tony Currie Jobless – *Shoot!* (30th July 1983)

TC Is Mastermind at Goole – *Green 'Un* (10th October 1983)

Currie Shows All His Old Skill – *Green 'Un* (17th October 1987)

Tony Turns the Corner – *Ranger Magazine* (circa 1993)
The Leeds Legends: Tony Currie – *Leeds United Official Monthly Magazine* (February 1995)
A Kiss in Time – *Action Replay* (December 1996)
Alan Birchenall and Tony Currie Exclusive on the 30th Anniversary of Their Smacker – *The Sun* (22nd December 2004)
Currie Still Simmering – by Rick Broadbent – *The Times* (24th July 2006)

Books
Jock Stein: The Definitive Biography – by Archie MacPherson – published by Highdown Books
Bring Back the Birch: The Alan Birchenall Story – by Alan Birchenall with Paul Mace – published by Polar Publishing
Football In Sheffield – by Percy M. Young – published by Dark Peak
Eddie Gray: Marching on Together – My Life with Leeds United – by Eddie Gray – published by Hodder and Stoughton
Joe Jordan: Behind the Dream – by Joe Jordan – published by Hodder and Stoughton
Jimmy Greaves: The Heart of the Game – by Jimmy Greaves – published by Time Warner Books
Stan Bowles: The Autobiography – by Stan Bowles – published by Orion Books
Looking For Eric: In Search Of the Leeds Greats – by Rick Broadbent – published by Mainstream Sport
The Mavericks: English Football When Flair Wore Flares – by Robert Steen – published by Mainstream Sport
The Leeds United Story – by Martin Jarred and Malcolm Macdonald – published by Breedon Books
A Passion for the Game: Real Lives in Football – by Tom Watt – published by Mainstream Publishing

Blades Tales – Memories of Supporting Sheffield United – edited by Matthew Bell, Kevin Titterton, Howard Holmes and Karen Keenan – published by Juma

And We've Had our ups and downs – 100 years – Leeds United and Leeds City 1905:2005 – by David Saffer and Gary Shepherd – published by Vertical Editions

Match of My Life – Sheffield United: Twelve Stars Relive Their Favourite Games – edited by Nick Johnson – published by Know the Score Books

Right Back to the Beginning – by Jimmy Armfield – published by Headline Book Publishing

Peter Shilton: My Autobiography – by Peter Shilton – published by Orion

Biting Talk: My Autobiography – by Norman Hunter – published by Hodder & Stoughton

Don Revie: Portrait of a Footballing Enigma – by Andrew Mourant – published by Mainstream Sport

Blade Runners: Lives in Football – by Gary Armstrong – published by Hallamshire Publications Ltd

Sheffield Football: A History Volume II – by Keith Farnsworth – published by Hallamshire Publications Ltd

Manchester United: The Quest for Glory 1966–1991 – by Tommy Docherty – published by Sidgwick & Jackson

The Sun Soccer Annual 1973 – edited by Frank Nicklin – published by World Distributors

All White – Leeds United's 100 Greatest Players – by John Howe and Andrew Dalton – published by Pitch Publishing

Sheffield United: Thirty Memorable Games from the Seventies – by Nick Udall – published by DB Publishing

Newspapers
Various issues of the *Montreal Gazette, The Calgary Herald, The Green 'Un, The Toronto Star, The Sheffield Star* and *The Yorkshire Post*.

Club Career Statistics

Watford

Season	League		FA Cup		League Cup	
	Apps	*Goals*	*Apps*	*Goals*	*Apps*	*Goals*
1967/68	17(1)	9	2	-	-(1)	-

Sheffield United

Season	League		FA Cup		League Cup	
	Apps	*Goals*	*Apps*	*Goals*	*Apps*	*Goals*
1967/68	13	4	-	-	-	-
1968/69	35	4	-(1)	-	1	-
1969/70	42	12	2	-	2	-
1970/71	42	9	1	-	2	1
1971/72	38	10	1	-	5	1
1972/73	39	1	2	-	5	1
1973/74	29	6	1	1	1	-
1974/75	42	7	2	1	4	-
1975/76	33	1	1	-	2	-
Total	**313**	**54**	**10 (1)**	**2**	**22**	**3**

Leeds United

Season	League		FA Cup		League Cup	
	Apps	*Goals*	*Apps*	*Goals*	*Apps*	*Goals*
1976/77	35	1	5	-	1	1
1977/78	35	3	1	-	5	1
1978/79	32	7	3	-	7	3
Total	**102**	**11**	**9**	**0**	**13**	**5**

Queens Park Rangers

Season	League		FA Cup		League Cup	
	Apps	Goals	Apps	Goals	Apps	Goals
1979/80	27(1)	3	1	-	4	1
1980/81	31	1	1	-	3	-
1981/82	20	1	7	-	1	-
1982/83	1(1)	-	-	-	-	-
Total	**79(2)**	**5**	**9**	**0**	**8**	**1**

Torquay United

Season	League		FA Cup		League Cup	
	Apps	Goals	Apps	Goals	Apps	Goals
1983/84	9	-	-	-	-	-
1984/85	5	1	2	-	-	-
Total	**14**	**1**	**2**	**-**	**-**	**-**

Career

	League		FA Cup		League Cup	
Total*	**525(3)**	**80**	**32(1)**	**2**	**43(1)**	**9**

* Currie also played in 5 Watney Cup matches (scoring 4 goals), 7 Texaco Cup fixtures (scoring 3 goals) and two Anglo-Scottish Cup games – all for Sheffield United.

Currie also appeared six times for Toronto Nationals in the CPSL scoring once.

International Record

England youth – 3 games
England Under 23 – 13 games, 4 goals
Full – 17 games, 3 goals (in the games below marked *)

England appearances
v Northern Ireland, Wembley (23 May 1972) – England
   lost 1-0
v USSR, Moscow (10 June 1973) – England won 2-1
v Italy, Turin (14 June 1973) – England lost 2-0
v Austria, Wembley (26 September 1973) – England
   won 7-0*
v Poland, Wembley (17 October 1973) – England drew
   1-1
v Italy, Wembley (14 November 1973) – England lost
   1-0
v Switzerland, Basle (3 September 1975) – England won
   2-1
v Brazil, Wembley (19 April 1978) – England drew 1-1
v Wales, Cardiff (13 May 1978) – England won 3-1
v Northern Ireland, Wembley (16 May 1978) – England
   won 1-0*
v Scotland, Hampden Park (20 May 1978) – England
   won 1-0
v Hungary, Wembley (24 May 1978) – England won
   4-1*
v Czechoslovakia, Wembley (9 November 1978) –
   England won 1-0

v Northern Ireland, Wembley (7 February 1979) –
England won 4-0

v Northern Ireland, Belfast (19 May 1979) – England
won 2-0

v Wales, Wembley (23 May 1979) – England drew 0-0

v Sweden, Stockholm (10 June 1979) – England drew 0-0